D1707158

RUBY KEELER

RUBY KEELER

A Photographic Biography

by
NANCY MARLOW-TRUMP

McFarland & Company, Inc., Publishers
Jefferson, North Carolina, and London

Frontispiece: Ruby Keeler, 1932

Cover: Publicity shot of Ruby Keeler for *42nd Street* (1933).

British Library Cataloguing-in-Publication data are available

Library of Congress Cataloguing-in-Publication Data

Marlow-Trump, Nancy.
    Ruby Keeler : a photographic biography / by Nancy Marlow-
Trump.
      p.   cm.
    Filmography: p.
    Includes index.
    ISBN 0-7864-0524-4 (case binding : 50# alkaline paper) ∞
    1. Keeler, Ruby. 2. Motion picture actors and actresses—
United States—Biography. 3. Dancers—United States—
Biography.
    I. Title.
PN2287.K48M37   1998
791.43'028'092—dc21   98-12992
[B]   CIP

©1998 Nancy Marlow-Trump. All rights reserved

*No part of this book may be reproduced or transmitted in any form or by
any means, electronic or mechanical, including photocopying or
recording, or by any information storage and retrieval system, without
permission in writing from the publisher.*

Manufactured in the United States of America

McFarland & Company, Inc., Publishers
  Box 611, Jefferson, North Carolina 28640

To:

Robert Hughson Trump, husband and friend

Maureen Daly-McGivern, my mentor

the Keeler and Lowe families

And:

Margie Keeler-Weatherwax, to whom I offer
my special thanks for her invaluable contributions
of photos and memorabilia

David Kosmo, son-in-law, for his help and love

ACKNOWLEDGMENTS

I am grateful to the individuals and companies who granted permission to reproduce certain cartoons, newspaper clippings, and photographs in this book, including Margie Keeler-Weatherwax and the Keeler family; *Dance Magazine*; the Sterling/McFadden Partnership; King Features; the New York *Daily News*; Warner Bros. (especially Judith Singer); Turner Entertainment Co.; the *Hollywood Reporter*; Bantam Doubleday Dell; Max Factor, Inc.; AP/Wide World Photos; *Variety*; Time/Life Syndication; the Cunard Lines and Roy and Jackie Toaduff.

CONTENTS

PREFACE

In the early 1950s, I was introduced to a very beautiful lady named Mrs. John Lowe—once known on stage and screen as Ruby Keeler. We met at Lakeside Golf Club in Toluca Lake, California. Lakeside was known as the golfing "home" of many male celebrities, and a good woman golfer was a rare commodity. Ruby Keeler Lowe was a ten handicap. Since my handicap was thirty, I settled for Ruby's friendship and losing to her in the ladies' poker games at the club. We also produced and directed "golf musicals," in which I had the rare opportunity to tap dance alongside my idol. Her beautiful Irish family virtually adopted me. I was privileged to meet her darling mother, Nellie, and her sisters, Helen, Gertrude, and Margie.

After her very early retirement from show business, Ruby devoted her love, time, and tremendous energy to raising her children and grandchildren. But in 1970, at the age of 60, she made a remarkable comeback on Broadway. Her return to the New York stage in the revival of the musical *No, No, Nanette* was a triumph. I was in the front row on opening night, glowing with pride.

In 1974, a serious illness forced Ruby to leave *Nanette* and move to Rancho Mirage, California. She began her courageous struggle to recover from a near-fatal aneurysm. Her tremendous faith and determination to be well pulled her through her greatest challenge.

Ruby made Rancho Mirage her home for the remainder of her life. I visited her there many times and noticed those blue eyes never lost their sparkle.

Ruby Keeler Lowe passed away in 1993. Her last remaining sister, Margie Keeler-Weatherwax, helped me to withstand the loss of a dear friend. Margie disclosed a treasure trove of her sister's rare old press clippings, programs, and pictures. From a priceless old box came the inspiration to compile this book.

1

With encouragement from my husband, Robert Trump, and my mentor, Maureen Daly-McGivern, these pages began to take shape. Now they are here for the reader, who I hope will come to love Ruby Keeler as I do.

NANCY MARLOW-TRUMP
Santa Barbara, California
December 1997

CHAPTER 1

The Early Years, 1910–1928

"YOU'RE GOING OUT A YOUNGSTER, but you've got to come back a star," Warner Baxter told Ruby Keeler in the 1933 smash film hit *42nd Street*. Little did Baxter know that his scripted words were uncannily prophetic. The film propelled Ruby to stardom, and she went on to become the memorable leading lady of choreographer Busby Berkeley's best Warner Bros. extravaganzas.

Ruby's own life had a rags-to-riches theme. She was born in Halifax, Nova Scotia, of Irish-Canadian parents. Elnora (Leahy) and Ralph Keeler were born, raised, and married in Halifax and worked in a family-owned grocery store. Ruby was their second child, born on August 25, 1910.

With older brother Bill, two-year-old Ruby, and one-year-old sister Gertrude, the Keelers decided to move to New York City in 1912.

"We lived in Yorkville," Ruby said in an interview in *Dance Magazine* (November 1928). "Yorkville was on the East Side of New York, between First and Second avenues, from 66th to 70th streets. When I was old enough, I used to actually dance on the sidewalks of New York in the evenings with my sister Gertrude and brother Bill. The other kids would join us."

Many years later, younger sister Margie Keeler-Weatherwax recalled, "My father was an iceman and delivered ice for the Knickerbocker Ice Company. Remember, we didn't have refrigeration then. We were so proud of Poppa, because he became a U.S. citizen as soon as possible."

The Keeler family expanded. Along came Helen (1913), Anna May (1915), and Margie (1917). Dad Keeler raised his six children admirably, delivering ice from door to door. In a home video owned by one of Ruby's closest friends, Madelyn Fio Rito Jones, Ruby spoke of her early days in Yorkville: "I would roller skate up to 85th Street from 70th to buy those long loaves of French bread for Momma. The kids today don't know about the fun of doing things like that. I'd also take a large can from home and buy soup from one of the soup kitchens." Ruby went on to say how much she loved

PREVIOUS PAGE: *Ruby Keeler and her brother, Bill, having their picture taken astride a donkey on the sidewalks of New York. Ruby was only two years old, and Bill was five. The year was 1912; vendors were selling roasted chestnuts, and organ grinders showed off their pet monkeys. Notice the brownstone houses and horse-drawn cart in the background.*

This photo, also taken in New York in 1912, shows baby Gertrude reposing in splendor between her brother, Bill, and her older sister, Ruby. Mr. and Mrs. Keeler proudly sent this photograph to their friends and family in their hometown, Halifax, Nova Scotia.

Ruby's favorite picture of herself as the "star-spangled girl" with brother, Bill, as her trusty "scout," in 1916. All of the Keeler children's clothes and costumes were hand-made by their mother, Elnora Keeler.

A family portrait of the Keelers, taken in New York, 1917. Ruby is now seven years old. Elnora (or Nellie, as she was affectionately called by her children) and Ralph Keeler are pictured with Bill and Anna May (in second row), Helen and Gertrude (seated), and Ruby (standing in front of her father).

Ruby in 1918, wearing her First Communion point d'esprit *lace dress and veil, age eight. She attended St. Catherine's parochial school on 68th Street in New York. It was there Ruby's dancing talents were discovered.*

New York in those days: "The aldermen [council heads of their districts in the city] were really kind to their districts. They would give families beautiful gift baskets every holiday season—filled with a turkey and nuts and fruit. The local police stations would also contribute." With a hearty, spontaneous giggle, Ruby added: "We cheated. Brother Bill would go to the police station, and I would get the alderman's basket. Momma would tell us we were wrong, but always added, 'We're all born with a little larceny in our hearts.' We'd have wonderful holiday dinners."

On the video, Ruby was asked how she dressed in those days. "It was no big deal then," she said. "If our hair was clean, the kids in back of us at school couldn't see any lice! Don't forget, we were poor and didn't know any rich kids."

Ruby's first schooling was at St. Catherine of Siena's parochial school on East 68th Street. In 1928 Ruby told *Dance Magazine*, "Once a week, Miss Helen

Ruby at age eight, 1918.

Guest came to our school to teach us 'drill.' These were classes in rhythmical exercise conducted to music.... Miss Guest would teach us folk dances like the Highland Fling, Sailor's Hornpipe and the Irish Jig." Many years later, Ruby recalled in the home video that Miss Guest thought she was talented and told Mrs. Keeler. (In later years, her sister Margie said it was one of the nuns, rather than Miss Guest, who alerted Mrs. Keeler to Ruby's talent.) "From then on," Ruby said, "I went to her studio every Saturday, and she also taught me ballet." The Keelers paid five cents a week for her lessons. Ruby said she loved going to class, partly because Miss Guest's studio was located within the Metropolitan Opera House building. "I loved the opera house. It was beautiful."

Ruby went on to learn the popular dances of the 1920s, which she performed at local community functions. She did so well, and her talent was so obvious, that the Keelers enrolled her in the Professional Children's School in New York. In her class were a few other children destined to become famous. Among them were

THIS PAGE: *Ruby (right) and Marjorie Holm, featured in "Ballet Classique," Helen Guest Dance Studio recital, 1921.*

OPPOSITE: *Ruby (right) and unidentified friend in "Highland Fling," dance recital, 1921.*

PROFESSIONAL
CHILDRENS' SCHOOL

Kely

MERTON of the MOVIES
CORT THEATRE APR 12

LEFT: *Program from* Merton of the Movies, *Cort Theatre, 1922.* BELOW: *Partial cast from* Merton of the Movies. *Ruby is third from left in the third row. Seated front row center with pipe and moustache is Tom Brown. Brown played juvenile leads in many films of the '30s and was always the very nice "boy next door." He emerged in the '60s as a villager in the long-running television series* Gunsmoke. *Back row center with beard is Gene Raymond (with beard). Raymond was an early child star and a leading man in the '30s. He later married singer-actress Jeanette MacDonald.*

Grand Christmas Kiddie Show

Jack Blue's Foolish Follies

Wilson Theatre

West New York's
Most Popular Theatre

DEC. 27-28-29-30

In conjunction with regular Feature Pictures
Every Afternoon and Evening

CLASSES
in Stage and
Ball Room
Dancing

ACTS
Written
—and—
Produced

JACK BLUE, Producer

Formerly Dancing Master for GEO. M. COHAN,
ZIEGFELD FOLLIES, and Others

Office & Studio, **233 West 51st Street,** New York City

CIRCLE 6136

Program from "Jack Blue's Foolish Follies," 1923.

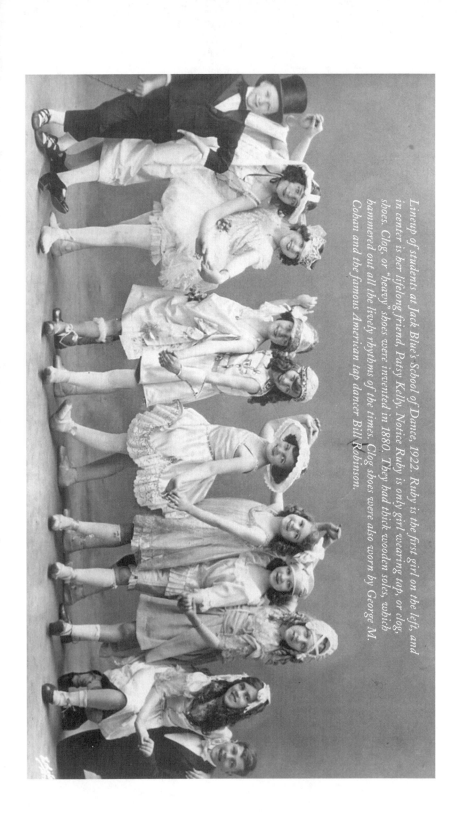

Lineup of students at Jack Blue's School of Dance, 1922. Ruby is the first girl on the left, and in center is her lifelong friend, Patsy Kelly. Notice Ruby is only girl wearing tap, or clog, shoes. Clog, or "heavy" shoes were invented in 1880. They had thick wooden soles, which hammered out all the lively rhythms of the times. Clog shoes were also worn by George M. Cohan and the famous American tap dancer Bill Robinson.

Ruby Keeler (left) and Patsy Kelly.

Patsy Kelly and Bill Keeler.

(continued from page 9) Lillian Roth, Marguerite Churchill, William Janney, Gene Raymond, and Tom Brown. (School patrons, one notes today on perusing old programs from performances, included Mrs. Charles C. Auchincloss, Mrs. Andrew Carnegie, Mrs. Edwin Gould, Mrs. J. West Roosevelt, Mrs. Percy A. Rockefeller, and Mrs. E. Henry Harriman.)

Among Ruby's performances at this school was a non-dancing role in the George S. Kaufman play *Merton of the Movies*. All the students appeared in this play, which was performed as a benefit matinee at the Cort Theatre in April 1922.

When Ruby was 12, the Keelers enrolled her in the Jack Blue School of Rhythm and Taps for five cents a class. Producer Blue was the former dancing master for famous song and dance man George M. Cohan, the dapper American actor, singer, and author-composer of many vaudeville and Broadway hits from the 1890s until his death in 1942. Ruby said of Blue (*Dance Magazine*, 1928), "Jack Blue is a wonderful instructor for my sort of work. He's taught me everything I know and made it fun—real fun."

In 1923, Ruby appeared in "Jack Blue's Foolish Follies" at the Wilson Theatre on the West Side of New York. Blue's show was run in conjunction with the regular feature picture of the day. "Foolish Follies" was billed as a "Grand Christmas Kiddie Show," and Ruby made her appearance in two numbers. Blue listed her on the program as "a coming star" and the girl "who can out-buck dance Georgie Cohan himself."

While enrolled at Jack Blue's, Ruby met a girl named Patsy Kelly. The two were destined to be lifelong best friends, and Patsy, too, would enjoy great success as a performer. Her career often had her appearing as the dumpy, frightened maid or the perennial wisecracking comedienne. Her film career started in 1933, when she appeared in *Going Hollywood*. She would share Keeler's smash comeback success in the 1971 revival of *No, No, Nanette*. Kelly successfully mixed motion pictures, Broadway shows, and television until her death in 1981.

Patsy Kelly and Ruby's brother, Bill, were also the best of buddies. Bill was an excellent dancer. His sister Margie says of her brother, "Bill and Ruby were the dancers in the family. They taught the rest of us. It was cheaper that way."

Margie says that her parents, in their youth, won many

amateur ballroom dancing contests in their native Halifax, Nova Scotia. Margie says, "Momma and Poppa always encouraged us and loved to have us dance."

(Bill Keeler went on to dance in vaudeville but eventually retired from show business. In 1936, he moved to California and became an assistant director at RKO Studios.)

At Jack Blue's, Ruby's star really began to shine. Another friend at Blue's told her of an opening in the chorus of a George M. Cohan production, *The Rise of Rosie O'Reilly*. Lying about her age (she was 13), Ruby auditioned and was hired for $45.00 a week—her first professional dancing job.

"I couldn't believe I'd be making so much money," Ruby said. "When I told Momma, she was so pleased. It was then she decided she'd walk me back and forth to the theatre. How she managed to do that and raise six kids, I'll never know," Ruby added.

Ruby had only three months of dance instruction before appearing in the chorus of *Rosie O'Reilly*. The show featured Mary Lawlor as the ingenue lead and George Bancroft as the villain.

While she was appearing in the show, New York impresario Nils Thor Granlund was trying to get some publicity for a new nightclub he was opening. He invited all the chorus girls from *Rosie O'Reilly* to compete in a beauty and dancing contest. Naive at age 13, Ruby wore a long, black velvet dress and her white buck tap shoes. She lost out in the beauty contest to another young lady named Ruby—a Ruby Stevens, who would later change her name to Barbara Stanwyck and become one of Hollywood's most prestigious actresses. (Also in the competition that night, and in the *Rosie* chorus line, was Mae Clarke, who would also go on to a Hollywood career. Today she may be best remembered for having a grapefruit shoved into her face by James Cagney in the film *Public Enemy*.)

There was no competition in the dancing department. Ruby's white buck shoes and nimble feet easily beat out the others. Granlund got his publicity, but neither Ruby Keeler nor Ruby Stevens received a prize from the gregarious Nils Thor Granlund.

During the run of *Rosie O'Reilly*, Ruby's talent and beauty caught the eye of director Earl Lindsay, a discerning young man who would later become a dance director for Paramount Studios. Lindsay offered Ruby a two-year contract, at $75.00 a week, to dance at the Strand Hotel Roof Garden. Ruby accepted and, along

Chorus girl Ruby Keeler.

Ruby Keeler in chorus-girl costume.

with Ruby Stevens (Barbara Stanwyck) and Mae Clarke, was soon hoofing at the Strand Roof.

Nils Granlund once again entered Ruby's life. He'd been watching her popularity rise at the Strand. Her innocence and youthful enthusiasm, along with her nimble feet, made her a favorite with the audience.

Ruby said, in an early interview, "Lord knows I certainly wasn't Granny's [Granlund's] type. He loved the tall, buxom, glamorous chorus girl. I wasn't a beauty, but he hired me, anyway, to dance at the El Fey club."

The El Fey, at 105 West 45th Street, was run by Larry Fey, and the club was rapidly becoming the most famous and notorious night spot in the country. The reason for its success was the presence of the most popular hostess on Broadway in the 1920s. Texas Guinan, Ruby said of her "boss," "Texas was very kind to me and protected me because of my age. I didn't even know what a gangster was!" (*Films in Review.*)

Texas had a unique ability to feel the pulse of her audience and use that as her guideline. Celebrities and prominent socialites flocked to her club. Guinan either had the crowd cheering or would quiet them down with a look or a sign—a sharp "shhh" gesture with her hand.

Her famous introduction for her "girls" was, "Give this li'l girl a great big hand." If the customers didn't listen, Guinan would shout, "Shut up! This li'l girl is gonna sing now." Then there would be complete silence. Guinan admitted she didn't know the secret of her success. She believed people knew she was sincere and instinctively felt she wanted them to have a good time.

The following are a few 1920s quotes describing Guinan:

"Texas Guinan is the world's perfect pacifier."

"The most talked of figure in New York night life."

"A Lady Ringmaster."

Not bad for a li'l gal from Texas, and in Guinan's words, "I see no end to the fun in my life, as long as the crowds give me a great big hand. I expect to beat Sarah Bernhardt's endurance." She added finally, "They'll have to padlock my coffin if they expect to keep me in it." (*Pictures* magazine, September 1926.)

Democracy and good fellowship were her standards. Guinan entertained princes, dukes, theatrical stars, society leaders, and

Texas Guinan at her upright piano with her pet Pekingese dog on top and her pet performer, Ruby Keeler, seated on floor, strumming the ukulele.

In Pictures magazine, September 1926, Guinan said, "I dread the inevitable day when my greatest prize, little Ruby Keeler, whom I sincerely love and wish she were my own, will leave me to go the way of the others.... She's a beautiful girl and can certainly do a great buck-and-wing and Charleston."

On this 1926 photo Guinan wrote to her favorite, Ruby Keeler: "I am most grateful to you for your great work."

*Texas and her "girls." Right to left: Ruby Keeler, Texas Guinan, "Irish Darling"
Kitty Reilly, "Acrobatic Marvel" Mary Lucas, and wardrobe mistress from the El
Fey club. Above picture was originally in* Pictures *magazine, September 1926.*

blue-book millionaires. The elite rubbed elbows with thugs, cops,
ex-cons, and big-time gangsters—and loved it. Irving Berlin, Albert
Edward (the Prince of Wales, who reportedly allowed everyone at
El Fey to call him "Eddie"), Ethel Barrymore, Lord and Lady
Mountbatten, Florenz Ziegfeld, Pola Negri, the Vanderbilts, and
"Champ" Jack Dempsey were just a few of Guinan's patrons.

High tipping was the rule of the night for the big spenders,
and Guinan's girls just had to sing for their supper. Ruby received
$500 one night when millionaire Crane Garts breezed in. Garts was
from California and had just inherited several million. Garts

Easy Money

"*In the chorus I earned $35 a week. In the Night Club, where I do a song and dance, I got a $500 tip one night, and almost every week get tips of fifty or hundred-dollar bills!*"

Left—Texas Guinan, hostess of the famous El Fey night club.

Right—Ruby Keeler, who received a $500 tip.

Ruby's $500 tip was featured in this magazine spread.

watched Ruby do her buck-and-wing, as did General John Joseph Pershing, commander of the American Expeditionary Forces in World War I. General Pershing, it has been told, stood at attention while Ruby did an encore to bugle taps.

Garts had a contest and bet $500 that no man in the club could out-buck-and-wing little Ruby. Up against comedians Joe Frisco and Franklyn Farnum, Ruby quickly and easily became $500 richer.

Looking back in an interview, Ruby said her youth and innocence, plus the fact that her mother walked her to and from the club, made her unaware of the dark side of the Prohibition years. "Dancing in speakeasies was just a job," she said. "None of us knew for certain who the bad guys were—nobody told us. Momma would always walk me home after the show. We thought nothing of strolling through the streets of New York at two in the morning." Ruby added, "How different New York was then."

And so went Ruby's career for a time. It was 1925, and Calvin Coolidge was the thirtieth president of the United States; actress Lillian Gish signed with Metro-Goldwyn-Mayer Studios for the largest salary ever paid an actress; pastel colors, large-brimmed hats, tailored suits, and shorter skirts were featured in the Easter Parade along Fifth Avenue.

Another major event making the headlines in the *Daily Mirror*, April 13, 1925, was the opening of Marcus Loew's newest motion picture theatre in Mt. Vernon, New York. Numerous Broadway stars and entertainers were appearing to celebrate the occasion. Ruby was on the bill—along with her little sister, Margie. Nils T. Granlund, who was now a radio announcer for station WHN, would be the Master of Ceremonies for the evening. Buster Keaton's new comedy, *Seven Chances*, was to precede the stage show.

Ruby was introduced as "the young, good-looking, live wire from the El Fey Club." As usual, she was a tremendous hit with the sophisticated audience, performing the Charleston and a "hard-shoe" tap dance.

The audience went wild when Granlund introduced little Margie; accompanied, of course, by Momma. Ruby stood back, leaned on the piano and watched her baby sister with love and pride.

Margie, who was eight years old at the time, was bestowed with a special nickname during this show. In an interview with this author, she explained: "When Mr. Granlund introduced me, he sort of gave me a little shove in the behind with his shoe. The audience roared, and he said to them, 'Here's Ruby's baby sister, little Kick-in-the-Pants'." Margie then proceeded to do her imitation of dancer Pat Rooney, and a Charleston that brought the house down.

Her diminutive size charmed the audience—but so did her talent. "Dancing talent just ran in our family," Margie told the author. "We all loved it, and it became a hobby. I always wanted to be good, but I never desired a career in show business."

Margie said her favorite place to perform was Palisades Park, New Jersey. "We'd drive there on Saturdays, go on all the rides, and appear in the stage show at night." Margie's eyes danced as she continued: "Outside of Ruby, I was the best dancer among the girls." Sisters Helen and Gertrude always said, "We were too short to fit in with those tall, willowy showgirls."

For the Loew's Theatre opening in Mount Vernon, N.Y., Doc Rankin's "Penshots" featured the "Girls from Texas Guinan's Del [sic] Fey Club." At the beginning of line of girls (on right) are Ruby and her younger sister, Margie.

Margie Keeler inscribed this photo, "To my dear sister Ruby, the best dancer on Broadway."

In an interview in 1931, Helen and Gertrude bragged about their baby sister. "She's better than we are. The kid is really clever." Ruby continued to dance at the El Fey as well as another of Texas Guinan's hot spots, the 300 Club. In 1926 two prominent New York theatrical producers, Aarons and Freedly, offered her a part in *Tip Toes*, featuring Jeanette MacDonald and Eddie Buzzell. Ruby told her family she was very unhappy at the rehearsals because everybody was so unfriendly. She left the show before it even opened. A few weeks later, she accepted a job dancing at the Silver Slipper nightclub. The sensational comedy team of Clayton, Jackson, and Durante was starring in the show, and the place was packed for every performance. Ruby's popularity was growing, and she was continually improving and refining her dancing technique.

Director Earl Lindsay hadn't spoken to Ruby since she left the Strand Roof. When he spotted her at the Silver Slipper, however, he offered her a featured part in a new musical comedy, *Bye, Bye, Bonnie*. The show, with Ruby in it, opened at the Ritz Theatre in January 1927. Ruby was 16 years old.

Bye, Bye, Bonnie starred Dorothy Burgess as Bonnie with William Frawley, Louis Simon, Rudolph Cameron, and Bernard Cavanaugh appearing as the comedians. The reviews were good, especially Ruby's. Garreck, in the *Herald Tribune*, said: "'Bye, Bye, Bonnie,' the newest confection with tunes and girls, brought forth, as something to rave about, a little lady named Ruby Keeler. A couple of hoorays for Miss Keeler. It took her turn at step dancing to tie up the entire routine on two occasions." Garreck continued, "She pushes enough personality across the footlights to make her own personable self well worth the price of the entertainment."

Here are a few more kudos: "Her black bottom dance with taps caused a 'riot,' and she found herself famous. Keeler had only previously been known to night club frequenters." And, "Ruby Keeler is a show stopper! The nimble-footed tap dancer of 'Bye, Bye, Bonnie' has scored an individual hit, even against the competition of highly featured players. Her 'Tampico Tap' number is a highlight."

Ruby's musical comedy career was off and running, even though she once said, "I wasn't ambitious, and the newspaper attention surprised me." She accepted producer Charles Dillingham's offer to appear in his new musical comedy, *Lucky*. It

7
DAY
BALL

DANCING
Broadway at 51st Street
"America's Foremost Ballroom"

7
DAY
BALL

SEVENTH ANNIVERSARY
monday, January 25 to Sunday, January 31

Saturday, January 30th, 1926
PROGRAM
World's Greatest Hostess

Texas Guinan

And Her mob of Adorable Girls

from

TEXAS GUINAN'S "300" CLUB

with

1. Dorothy Sterling . . . . *New Discovery from Chicago A Real Sensation*
2. Ruby Keeler . . . . *Champion Charleston and Buck Dancer*
3. Mary Lucas . . . . *Acrobatic Marvel*
4. Kitty Reilly . . . . *The Irish Darling*
5. Elaine Palmer . . . . *Ziegfeld "Follies" of 1923*
6. The Williams Sisters . . . . *"Greenwich Village Follies"*
7. "Kick-in-the-pants" Keeler . . . . *Another sensation*
8. Ritchie Craig . . . . *The Versatile Boy-Everybody's favorite*

Roseland Ballroom Program, January 30, 1926. Number seven on program, "Kick-in-the-pants" Keeler, is Ruby's younger sister Margie.

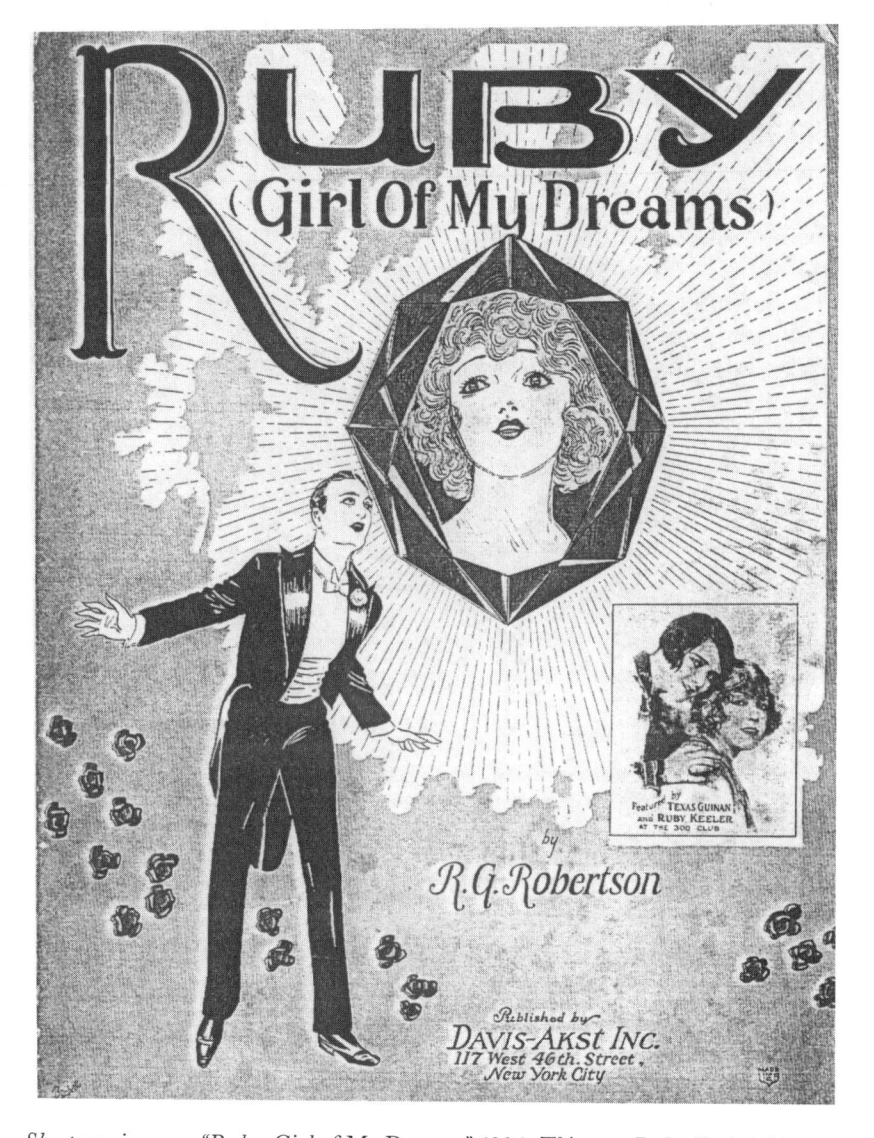

Sheet music cover, "Ruby, Girl of My Dreams," 1926. This was Ruby Keeler's hit
number when she appeared at Texas Guinan's "300 Club" in New York. Songwriter
R. G. Robertson must have been pleased to have this song pushed by Guinan and
Keeler.

Sheet music, incidentally, was invented in 1855. The only way song publishers
and writers could publicize their latest works was to hire a song plugger. These
gentlemen could be heard "tickling the ivories" in the most unlikely places—
Woolworth's Five and Dime, department stores, offices, and theatres.

Ruby Keeler in costume for Bye, Bye, Bonnie *(1927).*

would star Mary Eaton, but Ruby would have a featured dancing role.

Ruby once again scored a personal hit in *Lucky,* which opened at the New Amsterdam Theatre in March 1927. With Mary Eaton starring, the cast also included Walter Catlett, Richard (Skeet) Gallagher, Ivy Sawyer, and Joseph Stanley. *Lucky* was written by

elephone, Beekman 2000   NEW YORK AMERICAN—A Paper for People Who Think—WEDNESDAY, FEBRUARY 16, 192

Whirling Through 'Bye, Bye Bonnie,' with Dorothy Burgess and Ken Browne

In February 1927, the New York American published this cartoon-style review of Bye, Bye, Bonnie. Ruby is on right. To the extreme left is William Frawley, in one of his first Broadway musicals. Twenty-four years later, in 1951, Frawley became the harassed Fred Mertz in the classic I Love Lucy *television series.*

Otto Harbach, Bert Kalmar, Harry Ruby, and Jerome Kern. Another very famous name, directing the music, was Paul Whiteman. No wonder a prominent New York press cartoonist, Le Messurier, drew outstanding caricatures of the cast in *Lucky* with the headline: "You're Lucky to Get a Show Like 'Lucky.'"

A few "Ruby" revues: "Ruby Keeler is a little gem. She is showing real class."

"Ruby Keeler['s] … magnificent speed as a dancer is one of the advantages 'Lucky' enjoys." (*N.Y. Evening Journal,* February 22, 1927.)

"Little Ruby Keeler again scores with her tap stuff." (Le Messurier Cartoon, May 1927.)

Ruby loved the show. Even though it closed almost as soon as it opened, Ruby said, "We all thought it was far better than many of the shows which lasted longer." (*Dance* magazine, November 1928.)

The year 1927 was a big one for Ruby. Charles Dillingham immediately engaged her for *The Sidewalks of New York.* This lavish, costly musical was essentially a portrait of New York City— including orphans on the East Side, governor Al Smith, tenements, settlement houses, and misplaced babies. *Sidewalks* opened at the Knickerbocker Theatre, Broadway and 38th Street, on October 10, 1927. Ruby played an orphan named Mamie.

Copy of original sheet music from Lucky, *showing complete cast. Ruby is featured on lower right. She commented in an interview a few years later that* Lucky *didn't last long enough on Broadway. It was one of her favorite early shows.*

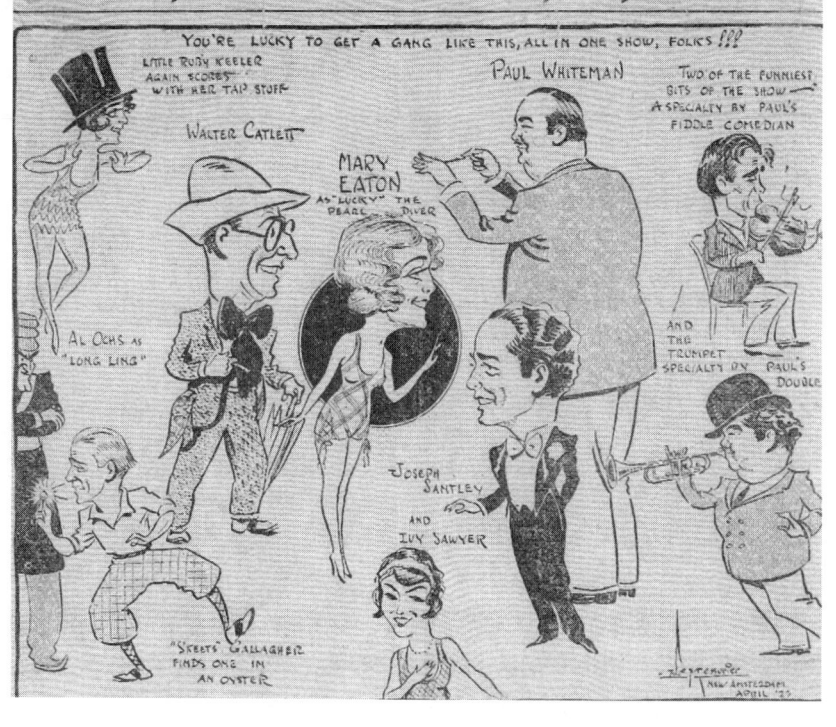

Cartoon by Le Messurier, unidentified New York paper, May 18, 1927. Caricatures of Ruby (upper left) and fellow cast members of Lucky.

Broadway audiences and the critics took notice of *Sidewalks*. Comedienne Ray Dooley was starred in Eddie Dowling's new musical. Rumor had it that Dowling (who wrote the book, lyrics, and music with Jimmy Hanley) tailored the show to fit Dooley's comedic talent but was overdoing it a bit—maybe because in private life, Dooley was Mrs. Eddie Dowling. No matter—even governor Al Smith and the honorable mayor James Walker loved the show.

Portraying one of the East Side gangsters in *Sidewalks* was an unknown named Lester Hope. It was his first Broadway appearance. We know him today as comedian Bob Hope, a major name in entertainment for 50 years.

With her dances directed by her ardent admirer Earl Lindsay, Ruby shone brightly. The Knickerbocker Theatre program described her as "an outstanding representative of the newer musical comedy

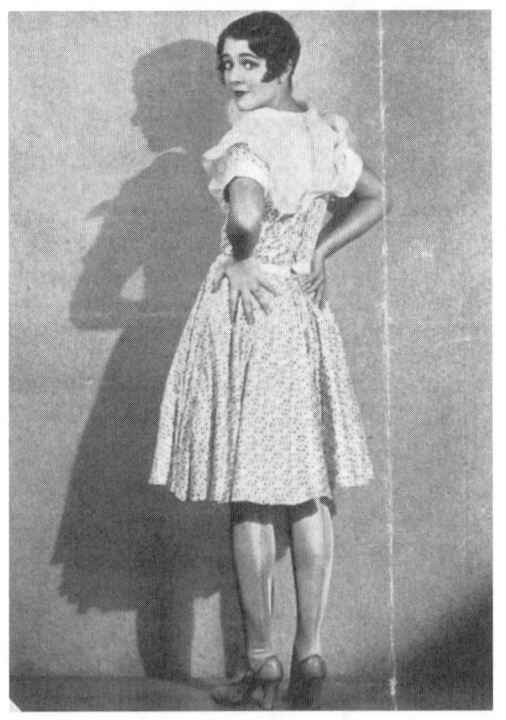

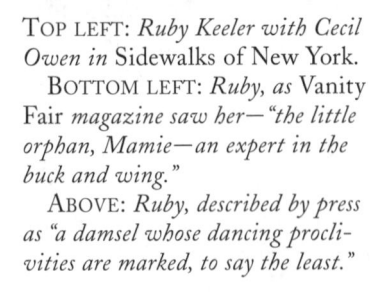

TOP LEFT: *Ruby Keeler with Cecil Owen in* Sidewalks of New York.

BOTTOM LEFT: *Ruby, as* Vanity Fair *magazine saw her—"the little orphan, Mamie—an expert in the buck and wing."*

ABOVE: *Ruby, described by press as "a damsel whose dancing proclivities are marked, to say the least."*

During the run of Sidewalks of New York, *Ruby (along with dance director Tom Nip) took time to help coach her sisters in the "Keeler Kicking Kwartette." From left to right are Margie, Anna May, Helen, and Ruby. The above picture is from Ruby's hometown of Halifax, Nova Scotia, whose population was proud of the success of their star.*

stars." Her reviews were extremely complimentary: "Dancing damsel divides honors with Ray Dooley. Last night's performance got under way largely under the influence of Ruby Keeler." "There was several lovely ensemble numbers, especially the Goldfish Glide, led by Ruby Keeler—a very capable and handsome dancer." "Keeler is an expert in the intricacies of the buck and wing and soft shoe stepping." (Unidentified New York paper column by Hans Stengel.)

"I liked appearing in *Sidewalks*," Ruby told *Dance Magazine* in November 1928, "because I was brought up in those kind of surroundings. I knew the kids and the life, and the show had a long run." She added, "We got to be one, big, happy family before the show closed. I loved my work, and I never got tired of doing the same thing over and over."

ABOVE AND OPPOSITE: *Two publicity shots of Ruby Keeler made during the run of* Sidewalks of New York, *1927.*

Ruby finished out the year with an unexpected honor when the press declared her legs among the world's finest. This may have resulted from a furor created in the American press when a Monsieur Poirer of France called American girls' legs "knob-kneed, grotesque, bulgy and generally ugly." A French dancer, Mlle. Mistinguette, was held to have the world's most beautiful legs, though the opinion is suspect as it was issued by Lloyd's of London, which insured Mistinguette's legs for one million dollars.

THE NEW YORK MAGAZINE PROGRAM

Knickerbocker Theatre
ABSOLUTELY FIREPROOF
REGNALRE AMUSEMENT CORPORATION
A. L. ERLANGER.....................................PRESIDENT
HARRY G. SOMMERS..................................MANAGER

FIRE NOTICE: Look around NOW and choose the nearest Exit to your seat. In case of fire, walk (not run)to THAT Exit. Do not try to beat your neighbor to the street.
. . JOHN J. DORMAN, Fire Commissioner.

WEEK BEGINNING MONDAY EVENING, OCTOBER 10, 1927
Matinees Wednesday and Saturday

CHARLES DILLINGHAM

Presents

RAY DOOLEY
—In—
EDDIE DOWLING'S
New Musical Comedy

"Sidewalks of New York"
Book, Lyrics and Music by
EDDIE DOWLING and JIMMY HANLEY
(The Writers of "Honeymoon Lane")
Staged by EDGAR MacGREGOR
Dances Staged by Earl Lindsay

CAST

MUGGSY		.HENRY DOWLING
MISS BROWN..⎫	Settlement Workers	⎧.....CAROLYN NOLTE
MISS SMITH...⎭		⎩WOODEY LEE WILSON
GERTIE, an orphan...		RAY DOOLEY
PARKER, superintendent of orphanage................		CECIL OWEN
THE GOVERNOR..............................		HARRY SHORT
MAMIE ....⎫		⎧.....RUBY KEELER
GLADYS ....⎬	Children of Orphanage	⎨....GLADYS AHERN
WILLIE ....⎭		⎩..WILLIAM AHEARN
BUCKLEY, manager of a garage......................		SAM MORTON
ABE COHEN ....⎫	Proprietors of	⎧.........JOE SMITH
MOE ZIMMERMANN.⎭	Coney Island Buses	⎩.......CHAS. DALE
A POLICEMAN....................................		EMILE COTE
THREE OLD TIMERS.....................		⎧.....JIM THORNTON
		⎨.JOSEPHINE SABEL
		⎩....BARNEY FAGAN
RUBY		RUBY KEELER
GLADYS		GLADYS AHERN
CARRIE		CAROLYN NOLTE
DOLLY		WOODEY LEE WILSON
ORGAN GRINDER..........................		EDWARD MAURELLI

The New York Magazine *program,* Sidewalks of New York, *October 10, 1927. Copy of original program, opening night of* Sidewalks.

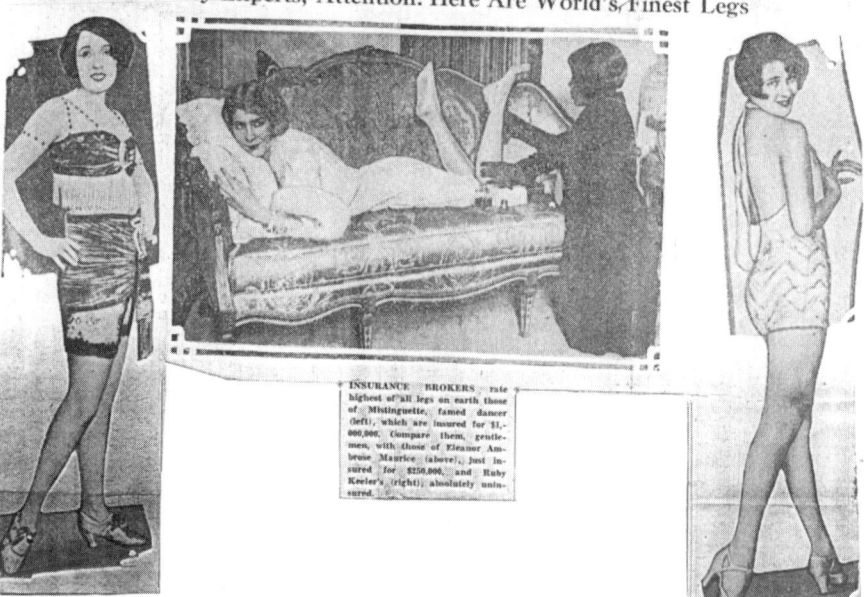

New York Evening Graphic, *December 1927. American dancer Eleanor Ambrose Maurice (left) insured her famous limbs for $250,000. French dancer Mlle. Mistinguette, (center) received massages on her million-dollar legs. The uninsured Keeler gams (right) speak for themselves.*

Ruby Keeler's legs were uninsured, but never uninspiring. On December 10, 1927, Ruby was featured alongside Mlle. Mistinguette and American dancer Eleanor Ambrose Maurice in a *New York Evening Graphic* photo spread. The headline read, "Beauty Experts, Attention! Here Are World's Finest Legs."

But *Sidewalks of New York* remained the most important event of 1927. During the run of that show, Ruby was noticed by two men who would play major roles in the future: Florenz Ziegfeld and Al Jolson.

CHAPTER 2

The Jolson Years, 1928–1939

In the summer of 1928, Ruby was offered a good part in Florenz Ziegfeld's *Whoopee*, a musical he was putting together to star the rolling-eyed entertainer Eddie Cantor and singer-actress Ruth Etting. (Etting's career was the basis for a 1955 film, *Love Me or Leave Me*, starring Doris Day and James Cagney.)

Ruby's life was about to change dramatically. Rehearsals for *Whoopee* weren't starting for several months, so she accepted an offer from the William Morris Agency to work on the West Coast. She and her friend Mary Lucas agreed to do a few "prologue shows," which the Loew Theatres put on before the movie feature.

Ruby also shot a two-minute short for Fox Studio. It was made to test the sound of tap dancing on film and to promote Fox's Movietone process. *Variety* reviewed the short and said, "Ruby Keeler snapped through a short but nifty tap dance. The machine gets every tap and reveals Miss Keeler as an exceptional female hoofer. Short but neat subject."

Ruby had already met one powerful man who would play an important part in her career—Florenz Ziegfeld. She soon would meet the world's highest-paid entertainer, Al Jolson, who would dominate her life for the next 11 years.

Many stories have been printed about the first meeting of this very famous couple. One version holds that Jolson saw Ruby at the El Fey Club and asked, "Who's the cute little tap dancer?" Ruby was 16 at the time and still largely unknown. Suddenly, one of the best-known entertainers in the world proceeded to sweep Ruby off her dancing feet. This version of the tale has Jolson showering Ruby with diamonds, furs, and baskets of flowers. It was even reported Jolson gave her a penthouse on Fifth Avenue and a pigeon-blood (dark red) ruby ring to match her name.

The truth is that Jolson saw Ruby in the Chicago run of *Sidewalks of New York* and never forgot her. When she disembarked from the train in Los Angeles, Jolson was at the station with Warner Bros. brass to meet famed comedienne Fannie Brice. He spotted Ruby immediately and asked for an introduction. Ruby said, in an interview for *Films in Review* (September 1971), "The

PREVIOUS PAGE: *Penn Station, New York City, 1918: Mr. and Mrs. Al Jolson departing for Los Angeles, California.*

An original drawing by "Barney Google" artist and author Billy DeBeck, sketched on the back of a menu from the Tavern Restaurant, West 48th Street, New York.

introductions were perfunctory, and everybody went their separate ways. That's the true story of how I met Jolson."

Al Jolson was born in Russia; most sources list his birthdate as May 26, 1886. His parents emigrated to the United States when he was seven and settled in Washington, D.C. His father was a rabbi, and as a youth, Jolson sang in his synagogue.

Margie Keeler-Weatherwax, Ruby's youngest sister, disputes Jolson's birthdate. "Al was the same age as our father when Ruby met him," she told the author. "Poppa was born in Halifax, Nova Scotia, in 1882. Al was 46 when he married Ruby, and she was 18."

There is no dispute, however, about Jolson's feelings for Ruby. He adored her youthful charm and innocence. He'd been married twice before, was more than twice her age, and was at the top of his career. When he appeared on the streets, thousands followed him and begged for autographs. Jolson, the greatest showman of his time, said in a 1928 press interview, "Ruby Keeler is an adorable kid. If there is a sweeter child in this world, I haven't met her."

Jolson and Ruby were married on September 21, 1928. Since Ruby was Catholic and Jolson was Jewish, the marriage was performed by a justice of the peace. The New York newspapers went

wild. The *New York Times* proclaimed, "Ruby Won in Conference," explaining that before Jolson, Ruby had been wooed by Johnny Irish, a close friend of heavyweight champion Gene Tunney. Irish later revealed that he gave Ruby up after a "conference" with Jolson. Irish had showered Ruby with many gifts, which he refused to take back.

The news cameramen swooped down on the newlyweds when they arrived back in New York. Actually, the press wanted pictures of "the dancing bride," but Ruby stepped behind Jolson and let him take center stage. She adored, admired, and respected her famous husband and always intended for him to be the "big shot" in the family.

WELL, AND HAPPY. LOVE.

Ruby and Jolson sent the radio message to Mother Keeler at her Woodside, New York, apartment. The newlyweds were sailing to Europe on the *Olympic* for a brief honeymoon. Ruby had to rush back for rehearsals of *Whoopee*, and Jolson had important appointments on the West Coast.

Nellie Keeler knew about the wedding plans long before the press did. Ruby and Al had told her they loved each other and always wanted to be together. When interviewed, Momma told the press, "For the first time, Ruby felt real love when she met Mr. Jolson. She asked me if I'd mind if she married him. I encouraged her, and I knew then the marriage would take place."

Ruby never made it to opening night of *Whoopee* on Broadway. There were conflicting stories as to why she quit the show after the out-of-town tryouts, even though she received excellent notices. It was reported she returned to California with Jolson at his insistence. Some of the press stated she left because of a "joking" reference to her marriage which had been inserted into the play's dialogue. Ziegfeld denied it, and certainly he held no grudge against Ruby. He offered her a good role in his next musical, *Show Girl*, which would open on Broadway the following year.

Whatever the reason, Ruby followed her husband to Los Angeles.

OPPOSITE: *A "Barney Google" cartoon dated January 16, 1928. (Reprinted with special permission of King Features Syndicate.)*

Italy, September 1928: The Jolsons enjoying an al fresco breakfast on their honeymoon.

Friends and family speculated on Jolson's character traits and what kind of a husband he would be. Ruby's sister, Margie Keeler-Weatherwax, told this author, "We didn't meet Al Jolson until Ruby returned from her honeymoon. They eloped, and it was a shock to the family. After we got to know him, we thought he was a wonderful family man. He liked and trusted us, which was unusual for him."

Margie said he loved Mrs. Keeler and did everything he could for the family. "He had a strange fixation, however," she added. "He wouldn't let Ruby go anywhere alone. One of us always had to accompany her even if it was New York or Palm Springs. The only thing she could do by herself was play golf!" She continued, "He was very jealous and possessive. He wouldn't let our boyfriends come to visit—just the family, period."

Two of Ruby's friends seemed to agree with Margie on Jolson's lack of trust and faith in anybody. Alice Faye Harris, leading motion picture actress of the '30s and '40s, didn't like the man at all. She told the author, "I met Ruby when she came on the set of *Rose of*

Newlyweds Mr. and Mrs. Al Jolson honeymooning in Europe, September 1928.

Washington Square, a movie I made in 1939 with Jolson and Tyrone Power. I immediately noticed she was very uncomfortable around him." She added vehemently, "I thought he was a pompous ass!"

Faye continued, "Jolson thought he was the greatest thing that ever happened, and he was a big star. Nobody's that big, and he seemed to intimidate Ruby." She added wistfully, "Ruby was such a darling girl. She had it all—a sweet, wonderful woman with the most beautiful blue eyes I've ever seen.... I wish I had known Ruby better, but I always felt as if I had been with her a thousand times. I was so comfortable around her—she was close to being an angel."

Although Ruby herself never talked much about her 11 years of marriage with Jolson, her very close friend Madelyn Fio Rito Jones (godmother to Al Jolson, Jr.) told the author, "Ruby had a sad life with Jolson. She was very young and impressionable, and he was one of the greatest stars of our time. He was terribly jealous of her and made her life miserable."

Jones pointed out that Ruby had worked since she was 13 years old, was extremely talented, and had become a star without any help from Jolson. She had a loving family and was always well protected from outside pressures. "We met in 1936, after I married bandleader Ted Fio Rito. Ruby was wheeling Al, Jr. in a baby carriage at our first meeting," Jones said. The two became inseparable friends and remained so until Ruby's death in 1993.

With her husband's approval, Ruby returned from California and opened in Flo Ziegfeld's newest musical extravaganza, *Show Girl*, on June 25, 1929. The show premiered at the Colonial Theatre in Boston, Massachusetts. A staff reporter for the *Daily Record* wrote, "The Battle of Bunker Hill was a minor event compared to the premiere of 'Show Girl.'"

Jolson insisted his wife be billed as Ruby Keeler Jolson. One review noted, "Al Jolson, the mammy-singing hubby of star Ruby Keeler, should be right proud of her. Just to help matters along, Al sat in the second row and sang 'Liza' while his wife danced. He also threw kisses at her and, along with his wife, shared wild applause from the capacity audience."

Show Girl received high praise when it opened in New York at the Ziegfeld Theatre, July 2, 1929. John Harkins of the *New York American* wrote, "In this musical comedy of abundance, Ruby Keeler is charming as she sings and dances.... Miss Keeler, newly risen to prominence, is admirably suited to the role of Dixie Dugan.... Ruby Keeler sings and dances her way to fame."

Once more, as he had in Boston, Jolson sang "Liza" from his front-row seat as Ruby was tap dancing on the stage. In the applause that followed, Jolson smiled and pointed to his heart. For the year 1929, it was a charming domestic scene.

Show Girl, with music by George Gershwin and lyrics by Gus Kahn and Ira Gershwin, was adapted for the stage by William Anthony McGuire from a novel of the same name by J. P. McEvoy. The McEvoy yarn was an unusual type of storytelling for the time. McGuire molded the male lead (played by Frank McHugh) into a faint caricature of his idol, famed columnist Mark Hellinger. The show was rich in all departments. Ziegfeld once again took an ordinary story, filled it full of pretty girls, and acquired the finest talent for acting, singing, dancing, and composing. Ruby Keeler Jolson, Eddie Foy, Jr., McHugh, Jimmy "Schnozzle" Durante with his partners Clayton and Jackson, and Frank Morgan fulfilled all of the above requirements. The *Broadway Theatre Guide* said, "'Show Girl' will be one of the foremost magnets for theatre goers for many months to come."

Among the women in *Show Girl* was a little-known dancer and singer, Dolores De Fina. De Fina changed her name to Dolores Reade, became a successful singer, and appeared in all the plush New York supper clubs in the 1930s.

In 1933, Reade met a young actor named Bob Hope. They were married three months later.

Dolores Reade Hope and the star of *Show Girl*, Ruby Keeler, were to remain good friends all through the ensuing years.

Ruby stayed with the show for only one month, after which she quit and was replaced by Dorothy Stone. Once more, excuses (poor health among them) were given for her rather sudden departure. The gossip held that Jolson wasn't happy with her success. Years later, Ruby explained to the press why Jolson insisted on a singalong while she was dancing on the stage. She said, "Al did stand up in the audience and sing ... but it was because he liked to sing; and when he felt like singing, he sang."

Whatever the reason, Ruby left a successful show and returned to Hollywood with her husband. She was not yet 20 years old.

The years between Ruby's departure from *Show Girl* (1929)

ZIEGFELD

THEATRE

Sixth Avenue at Fifty-Fourth Street
DAN C. CURRY, Resident Manager

FIRE NOTICE: Look around now and choose the nearest exit
to your seat. In case of fire, walk (not run) to
that exit. Do not try to beat your neighbor to the street.
JOHN J. DORMAN, Fire Commissioner.

BEGINNING TUESDAY EVENING, JULY 2, 1929
MATINEES THURSDAY AND SATURDAY

ZIEGFELD
"SHOW GIRL"
WITH
RUBY KEELER JOLSON
AND
CLAYTON, JACKSON & DURANTE

WRITTEN AND DIALOGUE STAGED BY
WM. ANTHONY McGUIRE
BASED ON THE NOVEL BY J. P. MCEVOY
MUSIC BY
GEORGE GERSHWIN
Lyrics by Gus Kahn and Ira Gershwin
Dances Staged by Bobby Connolly
Ballets by Albertina Rasch
SCENES BY JOSEPH URBAN
COSTUMES DESIGNED BY JOHN W. HARKRIDER
ORCHESTRA UNDER THE DIRECTION OF WILLIAM DALY
GENERAL STAGE DIRECTOR—ZEKE COLVAN
TECHNICAL DIRECTOR—T. B. McDONALD
PRODUCED BY FLORENZ ZIEGFELD

Copy of original Ziegfeld Theatre program for Show Girl, *1929.*
OPPOSITE: *The* Daily Mirror *carried this ad for* Show Girl *on Wednesday,
July 3, 1929. Ruby Keeler is at top right. At bottom right is Jimmy Durante (with
partners Eddie Jackson, left, and Lou Clayton). Durante got rave reviews, and*
Show Girl *was the springboard to his highly successful career.*

Show Girl

Introducing Noel Francis,
one of
Ziegfeld's loveliest.

Here's pretty
Barbara
Newberry,
graceful and easy
on the eyes.

Ruby Keeler was featured on the cover of New York Amusements *for the week of July 8, 1929.*

Ad for Show Girl *from the* New York Evening Journal. *Notice Ziegfeld's message to the public: "… it is up to the public to buy their seats at box office prices and prevent their falling into the hands of speculators."*

and her magnificent film debut in *42nd Street* (1933) are not well documented. For the most part she seems to have shied away from the public eye during those years, though her name appeared regularly in the press. (An interesting story from the *New York Evening Journal* dated May 29, 1930, describes how Ruby and

AMUSEMENTS

ROYALE West 45 St. OPENS TONIGHT 8:30
FIRST MATINEE SATURDAY
IRVING COOPER Presents

BOMBOOLA

A Red Hot Explosion of Colored
Entertainment in a Cool Theatre
GREAT CAST OF 70 PEOPLE

AMUSEMENTS

NEW AMSTERDAM, "The House Beautiful"
W. 42d St. Erlanger, Dillingham, Ziegfeld,
Managing Directors. Matinees Wed. & Sat.
ZIEGFELD Laughing Sensation

EDDIE CANTOR
"WHOOPEE"
458 SEATS AT $1.00

EARL CARROLL Thea. 50 St. & 7th Av
Mats. Thurs. & Sat.

Opens Monday Eve., July 1st
SEATS ON SALE TOMORROW
A New Annual Revue

EARL CARROLL'S

Sketch Book

Musical Volume of Laughs & Beauties by

EDDIE CANTOR
featuring
WILL MAHONEY—WILLIAM DEMAREST
and THE THREE SAILORS
56—PRIZE WINNING BEAUTIES—56

Ice Cooled CONNIE'S NEW SONG and DANCE HIT
HUDSON with BABY COX
W. 44th St. EDITH WILSON
Evs. 8:30, Mats. HOT "JAZZLIPS"
Thur. & Sat., 2:30 RICHARDSON

CHOCOLATES

HENRY MILLER'S Th., 124 W. 43d St.
Mts.Thurs.& Sat.2.30
EVENINGS AT 8:30

JOURNEY'S END

CORT THEA., W. 48 St. Evs. 8:50
Matinees Wed. and Sat.
THE

JADE GOD

NEW MYSTERY DRAMA

A SPARKLING NEW COMEDY
T
H 'TIRED' BUSINESS
E. MAN
GEO. M. COHAN 42 & B'way. Evgs. 8:50
Mts. Wed. & Sat., 2:30

"You're the Cream in My Coffee"

HOLD EVERYTHING!
MUSICAL COMEDY KNOCKOUT
VICTOR ONA BERT JACK
MOORE MUNSON LAHR WHITING
Broadhurst, 44 St., W. of B'y. Mts. Wed. & Sat.

REPUBLIC Thea., W. 42. Evs. 8:50
Mts. Wed. & Sat. 2:50

MY GIRL
FRIDAY! 5 TH BIG MONTH

JOHN GOLDEN Presents FRANCINE

Larrimore
in "Let Us Be Gay" By RACHEL CROTHERS
LITTLE, W. 44 St. Evs. 8:50. Mts. Wed. & Sat.

LONGACRE Thea., 48 St. W. of B'way.
Evs. 8:50. Mts. Wed. & Sat. 2:40.
Theatre Cooled by Iced Air

NICE WOMEN Newest Comedy Hit!
with Robert WARWICK & Sylvia SIDNEY

SELWYN SEATS ALL PERF.
Thea. W. 42nd $1.00 to $3.00
Mts. Wed. & Sat.
Will Morrissey's Comedy Revue

KEEP IT CLEAN

RONALD COLMAN
in "BULLDOG DRUMMOND"
GEO. WHITE'S W. 42 St. Twice Daily
2:45-8:45. Seats Mat.
APOLLO 50c, 75c & $1.00

ON WITH THE SHOW
2:45—8:45
EXTRA
6 P. M.
REFRIGERATED SHOW
WINTER GARDEN SUNDAY
B'WAY & 50TH ST.

THE FIRST ALL TALKING FARCE

"FALL OF EVE"
("La Chute d'Eve")
"IT'S NAUGHTY—BUT IT'S NICE"
A Columbia Talking Picture
AT THE EMBASSY B'way at 46th St.
COOL Tw. D'ly 2:15, 8:45

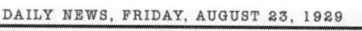

Daily News, *Friday, August 23, 1929. Ruby had already left the cast of* Show Girl *when she "starred" with Eddie Foy, Jr., in this newspaper cartoon. Foy appeared in* Show Girl *as a principle performer after the Foy family broke up their famous vaudeville act called "The Seven Little Foys." He was the son of American vaudeville comedian Eddie Foy, Sr., who kept the country laughing in the early 1920s. (In 1954, Bob Hope played Eddie Foy, Sr., in the filmed life story of the Seven Little Foys.)*

The above cartoon was "staged" by Mark Hellinger, as American journalist, who in the 1940s, turned writer-producer. (Copyright 1929. Reprinted by permission of Daily News, L.P.)

(continued from page 55) actress Marian Nixon were accosted by a lone burglar as they rode the *Santa Fe Chief* near Los Angeles. Ruby Keeler Jolson's screams were so loud, she alerted the entire train, and the bandit fled.) Many columnists reported Ruby receiving and turning down various screen offers, largely due to Jolson's popularity in pictures, but Ruby denied most of these stories.

Meanwhile, other members of the Keeler family were occasionally mentioned in the press. With sister Ruby married to Al Jolson, Gertrude and Helen Keeler were a headline act at the Orpheum Theatre in New Orleans. Both sisters were excellent tap dancers in their own right, and this was their stage debut.

Of their new brother-in-law, they said, "He's the biggest tease in the world. He likes to go to the 'icebox,' fix a huge sandwich on rye bread and eat it in the living room. You'd never know he was such a famous man."

OPPOSITE: *The Amusement section from the* New York Evening Journal *offered this list of the shows running on Broadway along with* Show Girl.

Al Jolson, 1930.

Another Keeler marriage took place this year. Brother Bill quit vaudeville, married Miss Charlotte Hoag, moved to California and became a stock broker.

42nd Street

One press release that the public believed and liked went as follows: Mr. and Mrs. Al Jolson went to the prizefights and sat next

Gertrude (left) and Helen Keeler, New Orleans Press, *1931.*

to famed producer Darryl Zanuck. He had seen a screen test Ruby had made for a Jolson film, and between rounds of the fight, he received permission from the Jolsons to review the test. The story had the perfect ending—Zanuck saw the test and signed Ruby the very next day for the ingenue role in *42nd Street* (1933).

Whether this story is true or not, two things are certain: *42nd Street* made film history, and so did Ruby Keeler. Busby Berkeley directed her in the most complex dance numbers ever seen on the screen, and Ruby's unique charm, talent, and refreshing personality delighted the critics and the viewing public. In spite of the popularity and importance of her husband, Ruby stole the spotlight. Her screen debut outshone his, thanks to her ingratiating appeal.

42nd Street was a tremendous hit for Warner Bros. Released on February 4, it was called "The Entertainment Miracle of 1933." Talking pictures were no longer an oddity in the growing film industry, and the public was ready for a truly remarkable musical.

The picture featured Warner Baxter, Bebe Daniels, George Brent, Una Merkel, Dick Powell, Ginger Rogers, Guy Kibbee, and Ned Sparks—plus 200 beautiful chorus girls in the lavish musical numbers. Famed choreographer Busby Berkeley went the limit on creating complex, dazzling, extravagant musical routines. His two important pieces for Ruby were the title number, in which she tapped on the roof of a taxi, and the now famous "Shuffle Off to Buffalo" tap routine.

Lloyd Bacon directed, and in an April 1933 interview with *Silver Screen Magazine,* he said Ruby was "probably the most outstanding personality to come to the screen since [Maurice] Chevalier. She has a new, fresh charm—utterly unlike anyone you've ever seen on the stage or screen. She can dance and act, and that combination is rare. Maybe I'm prejudiced, as her director, but I'd say Ruby has the most shining future of any new screen star. Al Jolson can prepare to share starring honors in the family when '42nd Street' is released."

Ruby, of course, was aware of the attention she was receiving in Hollywood and from the press around the country. She said before the preview of *42nd Street* (*Silver Screen,* April 1933)," I hope I'm good in the movie and that the fans will like me. Any girl in a thousand could have played the part, but I happened to get the break." The headlines in the press of Ruby's hometown, Halifax, Nova Scotia, read: "Halifax Keeler-Conscious." They said she was the "greatest screen find of the year" and that their hometown girl had attained a position in Hollywood for which other actresses had struggled for years.

Even president-elect Franklin Delano Roosevelt, joined in the Hoopla. Roosevelt extended to J. L. Warner, and to the motion picture industry in general, an invitation to attend his inauguration

OPPOSITE: *Left to right: Una Merkel, Ruby Keeler, and Ginger Rogers filming* 42nd Street.

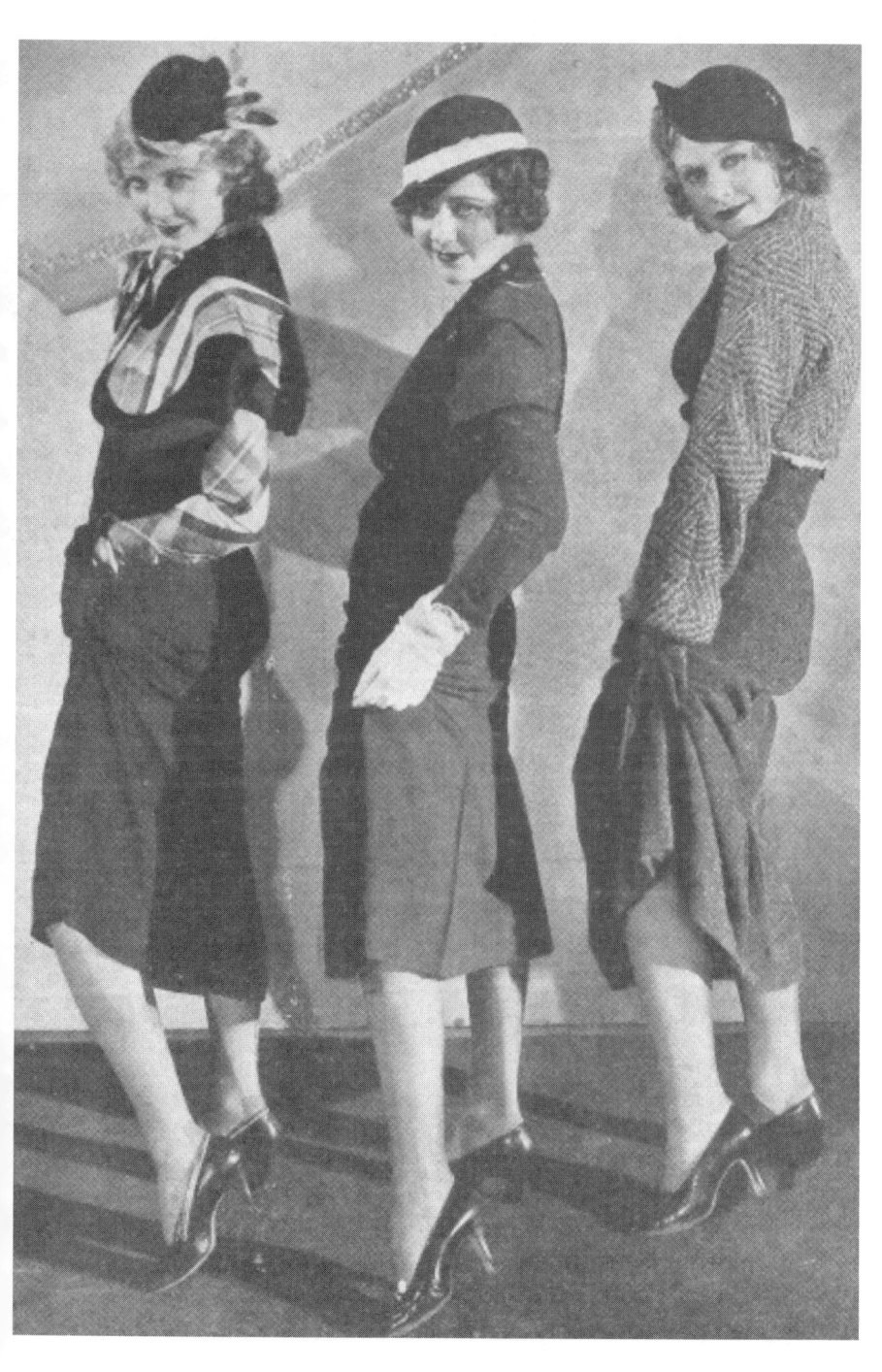

Left to right: Gertrude Keeler, Ruby Keeler Jolson, and Helen Keeler, 1932. The Keeler sisters at Warner Bros. during the filming of 42nd Street. *Ruby's two sisters were working as extras on the film to gain experience for contemplated screen careers.*

on March 4, 1933. The stars crossed the country to Washington in a special train known as the *42nd Street Special.* The entire delegation appeared in the inaugural parade, the first time motion picture stars took part in the inauguration of a president of the United States. Among the celebrities booked for the trip were Ruby, Bebe Daniels, Joe E. Brown, James Cagney, William Powell, George Brent, Warner Baxter, Bette Davis, Joan Blondell, Warren William, Guy Kibbee, Loretta Young, Douglas Fairbanks, Jr., Ginger Rogers, and Una Merkel.

The *42nd Street Special* left Hollywood on February 20, 1933. Jack Warner wrote to Democratic National Headquarters: "The film colony is firmly convinced March 4, 1933, will usher in a new era of better times, and we will try to spread that conviction on our way across the country. We expect that Hollywood's 'Better Times Trip' will be one of the most unique in the history of inaugural celebrations."

42nd Street opened at the Strand Theatre on March 9, 1933. Throngs jammed the theatre to applaud and cheer the contingent of

ABOVE THROUGH PAGE 67: *Glamour stills of Ruby Keeler Jolson taken during the filming of* 42nd Street.

famous Hollywoodites who had arrived on the *42nd Street Special.* They also found much to applaud on the screen. Bland Johaneson wrote in the *Daily Mirror* review (March 10, 1933), "'42nd Street' is a brisk, smart and cheery movie, distinguished by the film debut of the appealing little Ruby Keeler; a new, refreshing type to step before the jaded cameras of Hollywood."

The *New York Times* called the film "the liveliest and most tuneful musical to come out of Hollywood." Of Ruby, the *Times* said, "Her ingratiating personality, coupled with her dances and songs, adds to the zest of this offering. It's a film which reveals the forward strides made in this particular medium."

In fact, *42nd Street* set the pattern for film musicals for many years to come. Ruby said many years later, "It was a wonderful era, and those pictures, directed by Buzz Berkeley, will never be forgotten."

Golddiggers of 1933

To capitalize on the tremendous success of *42nd Street* and the magical team of Ruby and Dick Powell, Warner Bros. was determined to release *Golddiggers of 1933* as soon as possible. The studio spent months shooting five elaborate chorus numbers on "closed to the public" soundstages. The Warner pressbook said: "Give Ruby Keeler a special blurb whenever possible. Fan mail and

exhibition reports indicate that millions are waiting to see her again on the strength of her '42nd Street' performance."

Besides Ruby, the picture featured Warren William, Aline MacMahon, Joan Blondell, Ginger Rogers, Dick Powell, and Guy Kibbee. Ruby, Blondell, and MacMahon are three unemployed showgirls, and Powell is the rich young man posing as a struggling singer and composer. Mervyn LeRoy was engaged as dance director.

Golddiggers was actually photographed on two stages at once. LeRoy shot his scenes with one crew while Berkeley was on another stage photographing the spectacular dance numbers. When

PAGES 63–67: *Glamour stills of Ruby Keeler during the filming of* 42nd Street.

everything was finished, the two directors got together in the cutting room and assembled the picture.

42nd Street and *Golddiggers of 1933* started a new cycle of film musicals, mainly because Berkeley's visually extravagant and seemingly impossible dance routines dominated the screen. For the

As director Julian Marsh in 42nd Street, *Warner Baxter scolds Ruby Keeler.*

"Shadow Waltz" number in *Golddiggers,* as Dick Powell was crooning in the foreground, Berkeley's girls, with wires strapped to their bodies, played lighted violins. The outlined violins had an absolutely indescribable effect when all the lights were turned off on the set. Coincidentally, while the girls were up on the metal bridges, as high as 50 feet off the ground, the 1933 earthquake hit the Los

Collage of stills and review of 42nd Street.

ABOVE THROUGH PAGE 72: *Ruby Keeler (and co-star Dick Powell) were featured on many movie-magazine covers by the fall of 1933.*

Angeles area. Berkeley knew it was impossible to get the dancers down, so he continued shooting the number. As soon as the quake was over, Berkeley called "cut" and brought his girls down safely.

Huge silver dollars were the motif for the "We're in the Money" number. Ginger Rogers sang an entire chorus of the hit

PHOTOPLAY

The "NEW DEAL" In GIRLS

song in pig latin. Ruby said of Rogers in a studio interview, "I remember watching Ginger during the filming of 'Golddiggers,' and I knew then she'd be a star. She had the ambition and the drive I never had. I always felt there was more to life than show biz."

Of Busby Berkeley, Ruby said, "Buzz was so wonderful to work with. He knew what he wanted and always got it. All the girls loved

him, and some of them wouldn't take jobs after a Berkeley picture was finished for fear they wouldn't be in his next one."

Berkeley hired girls of every type—because, as he said, "some people like blondes, some like brunettes, some like girls thin, some like them plump. It's obvious to me no one girl can combine the

Dedicated to the greatest all-star cast of the month—and this means not only the "name" players, but the amazing chorus, the shapeliest and sprightliest ever seen on the screen

Left, Aline McMahon
Joan Blondell, and Ruth
Keeler, the three so
different heroines of the
big music-film.

Above, the charming romantic stars
of "Gold Diggers of 1933." Ruby
Keeler proves that her hit in "42nd
Street" was no accident. Dick Powell becomes head man of movie
musicals. Here is a boy with a real
voice, and that personality something that makes girls stay to see the
picture through twice.

Bouquets for Blondell, Keeler, Aline McMahon, Dick Powell—and all the other grand troupers who make "Gold Diggers of 1933", the top in entertainment!

Press material for Golddiggers of 1933 *shows Dick Powell and his glamorous ladies—Aline McMahon, Joan Blondell, and Ruby Keeler.*

ideal." So saying, he gathered together 107 delectable chorines for *Golddiggers*. A famous New York promoter saw them on the set and was so impressed, he signed them up en masse for his night club. He chartered a special train and, when the picture was finished, swooped them off to New York.

In *Golddiggers of 1933*, Hollywood glorified the American girl

Publicity collage from Golddiggers of 1933. TOP LEFT: *Ruby Keeler in white wig, Dick Powell with violin, and Busby Berkeley directing "Shadow Waltz" scene.* TOP RIGHT: Golddiggers *sweethearts—Ruby Keeler and Dick Powell.* BOTTOM LEFT: *Jealous Joan Blondell watching Dick Powell and Ruby embrace.* BOTTOM RIGHT: *Dick Powell with his "Bookends," Ruby Keeler and Joan Blondell.*
   OPPOSITE: *In this* Golddiggers *shot, Ruby is seen in another one of Busby Berkeley's imaginative collages. All of Berkeley's scenes were created through camera and cutting tricks. Here Ruby is pictured amid a vast array of New York skyscrapers.*

STRAND THEATRE
P R O G R A M
Wednesday October 4th, 1933
WORLD PREMIERE
Warner Bros. Pictures, Inc. presents

FOOTLIGHT PARADE

JAMES CAGNEY   JOAN BLONDELL
RUBY KEELER   DICK POWELL
Directed by LLOYD BACON
Numbers created and staged by BUSBY BERKELEY
Screen play by
MANUEL SEFF and JAMES SEYMOUR
Songs by
HARRY WARREN   AL DUBIN
SAM FAIN   IRVING KAHAL

SONG NUMBERS: "Shanghai Lil", "By A Waterfall", "Honeymoon Hotel", "Ah! The Moon Is Here", "Sittin' On A
Backyard Fence".

Chester Kent	James Cagney
Nan	Joan Blondell
Bea	Ruby Keeler
Scotty	Dick Powell
Gould	Guy Kibbee
Mrs. Gould	Ruth Donnelly
Vivian	Claire Dodd
Bowers	Hugh Herbert
Francis	Frank McHugh
Frazer	Arthur Hohl
Thompson	Gordon Westcott
Cynthia	Renee Whitney
Joe Grant	Philip Faversham
Miss Smythe	Juliet Ware
Fralick	Herman Bing
Appolinaris	Paul Porcasi
Doorman	William Granger
Cop	Charles Wilson
Gracie	Barbara Rogers

VITAPHONE SHORT SUBJECTS: "The Dish Ran Away With The
Spoon", "A Looney Tune Cartoon". Strand News Events.

Program for the world premiere of Footlight Parade *at the Strand Theatre, New York—October 4, 1933.*

OPPOSITE: *Ruby featured in the spectacular "We're in the Money" number, choreographed by Busby Berkeley for* Golddiggers of 1933.

FOUR OF THE 10 BIG STARS IN "FOOTLIGHT PARADE"

Left to right: Gertrude Keeler (Ruby's sister), James Cagney, and Ruby Keeler on the set of Footlight Parade, *September 1933. (Photo by Bert Longworth.)*
    OPPOSITE: *(Top to bottom:) Ruby Keeler, James Cagney, Joan Blondell, and Dick Powell of* Footlight Parade.

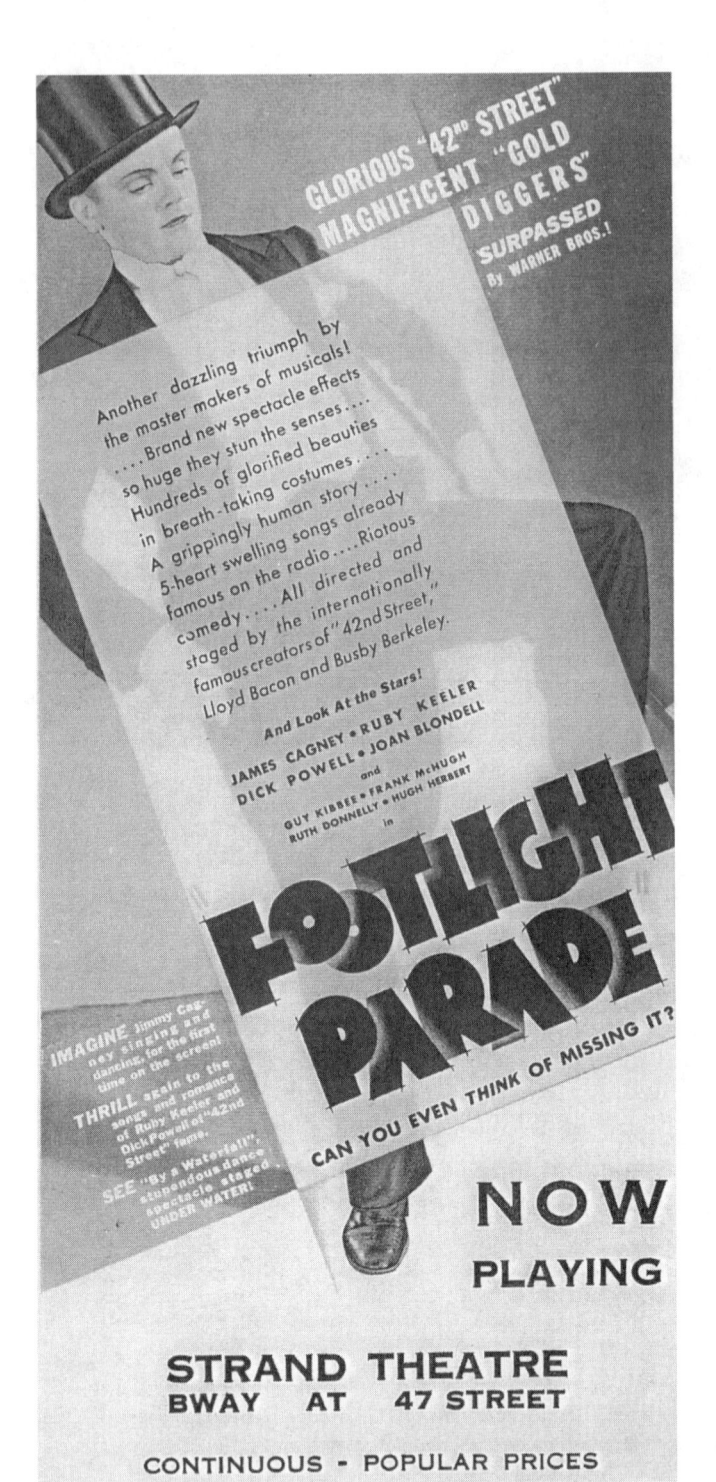

GLORIOUS "42ND STREET"
MAGNIFICENT "GOLD DIGGERS"
SURPASSED
By WARNER BROS.!

Another dazzling triumph by the master makers of musicals! ....Brand new spectacle effects so huge they stun the senses.... Hundreds of glorified beauties in breath-taking costumes.... A grippingly human story.... 5-heart swelling songs already famous on the radio....Riotous comedy....All directed and staged by the internationally famous creators of "42nd Street," Lloyd Bacon and Busby Berkeley.

And Look At the Stars!

JAMES CAGNEY • RUBY KEELER
DICK POWELL • JOAN BLONDELL

and

GUY KIBBEE • FRANK McHUGH
RUTH DONNELLY • HUGH HERBERT

in

FOOTLIGHT PARADE

IMAGINE Jimmy Cagney singing and dancing for the first time on the screen!

THRILL again to the songs and romance of Ruby Keeler and Dick Powell of "42nd Street" fame.

SEE "By a Waterfall", stupendous dance spectacle staged UNDER WATER!

CAN YOU EVEN THINK OF MISSING IT?

NOW
PLAYING

STRAND THEATRE
BWAY AT 47 STREET

CONTINUOUS - POPULAR PRICES

(continued from page 73) as not even Florenz Ziegfeld ever dreamed of doing. As one ad trumpeted, Warner Bros. would "surpass the glories of *42nd Street*" with "bigger stars, more gorgeous girls, more song hits," and an "even more lavish spectacle."

Footlight Parade

Warners lost no time in putting the sweethearts of the film musicals, Ruby Keeler and Dick Powell, together again. It would be their third film together, and for even more box-office insurance, Warners added James Cagney to the cast. Busby Berkeley was again hired to direct the musical numbers.

Keeler, Cagney, and Berkeley combined their talents, and *Footlight Parade* was a tremendous hit—"a massive achievement for all concerned" (Clive Hirschhorn, *The Warner Bros. Story*).

Cagney plays a Broadway producer who finds himself out of work with the arrival of talking pictures. He also realizes vaudeville is folding, musical comedies are losing their appeal, and people want "talkies." Legitimate theatres are being changed into picture "palaces." He decides to stage a series of "mini-musicals" to precede the screening of the feature film.

With the assistance of Ruby, Powell, and Joan Blondell, Cagney conquers fatigue, theatrical spies, conniving sirens, and greedy employers. He stages the film's famous finale—three back-to-back musical numbers including "Honeymoon Hotel," "By a Waterfall," and "Shanghai Lil." Berkeley's aqua-ballet in the "Waterfall" number was a spectacular achievement.

On Wednesday, October 4, 1933, the world premiere of *Footlight Parade* was held at the Strand Theatre in New York.

Dames

The September 1933 issue of *Screen Romances Magazine* had featured Ruby Keeler in a reader-response contest under the headline, "Dancing Lady or Dramatic Star?" The copy read,

OPPOSITE: *From the original program for* Footlight Parade. *The picture was Cagney's first singing and dancing role.*

Warner Brothers believe that Ruby Keeler has that same wistful, appealing personality that is embodied in Janet Gaynor. Warner Brothers believe that Ruby is now ready to step out of her dancing shoes and step into straight dramatic roles.

But they are anxious to do the thing that will please Ruby's many, many admirers. And here's the question they would like you to answer:

"Should Ruby Keeler give up her dancing roles for straight dramatic parts?"

Readers were invited to answer this question in 50 words or less, for a chance at one of the cash prizes offered by Warners.

Whether the responses truly influenced Warners or the studio made the decision on its own, it is worth noting that Ruby's singing and dancing dropped off in her next two pictures. Actually, filming for *Dames* (1934) was already complete by the time the *Screen Romances* article was published, which suggests the studio had its own plans long before the contest was announced.

Dames was Ruby's fourth picture with Dick Powell, and it wasn't as successful as her other film musicals—maybe because she had only one number in it, featuring the hit song "I Only Have Eyes for You" (written by Al Dubin and Harry Warren). Incidentally, many years later, Ruby told this author that it was one of her favorite songs.

Busby Berkeley was once again hired as dance director, but many of the reviews of the time stated that a great deal of film footage was given to Berkeley's staging of some of his lesser creations. *Dames* was Ruby's last film under Berkeley's supervision.

Flirtation Walk

Flirtation Walk (released November 2, 1934) was the first Ruby Keeler picture that did not carry the Warner Bros. name. However, First National, whose trademark the picture bore, was wholly owned by Warners, so Ruby had not switched employers. *Flirtation Walk* once again teamed the "musical lovers," Ruby and Dick Powell. The setting for this film musical is West Point Military Academy, and strangely enough, Ruby does not dance in this one. Her sister Gertrude, however, does appear in the chorus.

Ruby Keeler attending premiere of Wonder Bar, *starring husband Al Jolson, 1934. Left to right: Sister Gertrude Keeler, mother Elnora Keeler, Ruby, and her father, Ralph Keeler, at opening night in New York. The Jolson epic was a musical drama set in a Paris night club. Lloyd Bacon directed, and the movie featured Kay Francis, Dolores Del Rio, and Dick Powell.*

Ruby stated in an interview in 1968, "The early '30s were gloomy depression years, and Dick and I hope we brought some sunshine into peoples' lives."

Ruby plays an officer's daughter, and Dick Powell is a cadet who falls in love with her. Directed by Frank Borzage, the picture also features Pat O'Brien, Ross Alexander, Guinn Williams, and Henry O'Neill.

The year 1935 was an exciting, promising one for Mr. and Mrs. Al Jolson. They had two lovely homes, making their travels easier as they journeyed from coast to coast. Their Encino, California, ranch was the "home base"; but the residence in Scarsdale, New York, came in handy.

Sadly, 1935 also brought tragedy when Ruby lost her young sister Anna May. Born in 1915, Anna May was next to the youngest of the six Keeler children. In her childhood years, the family

"DAMES"

— Glorifying the American Chorus Girl

Above, one chorine plays "soldier," while another one plays "pirate"— to the music

Promotional material for Dames.

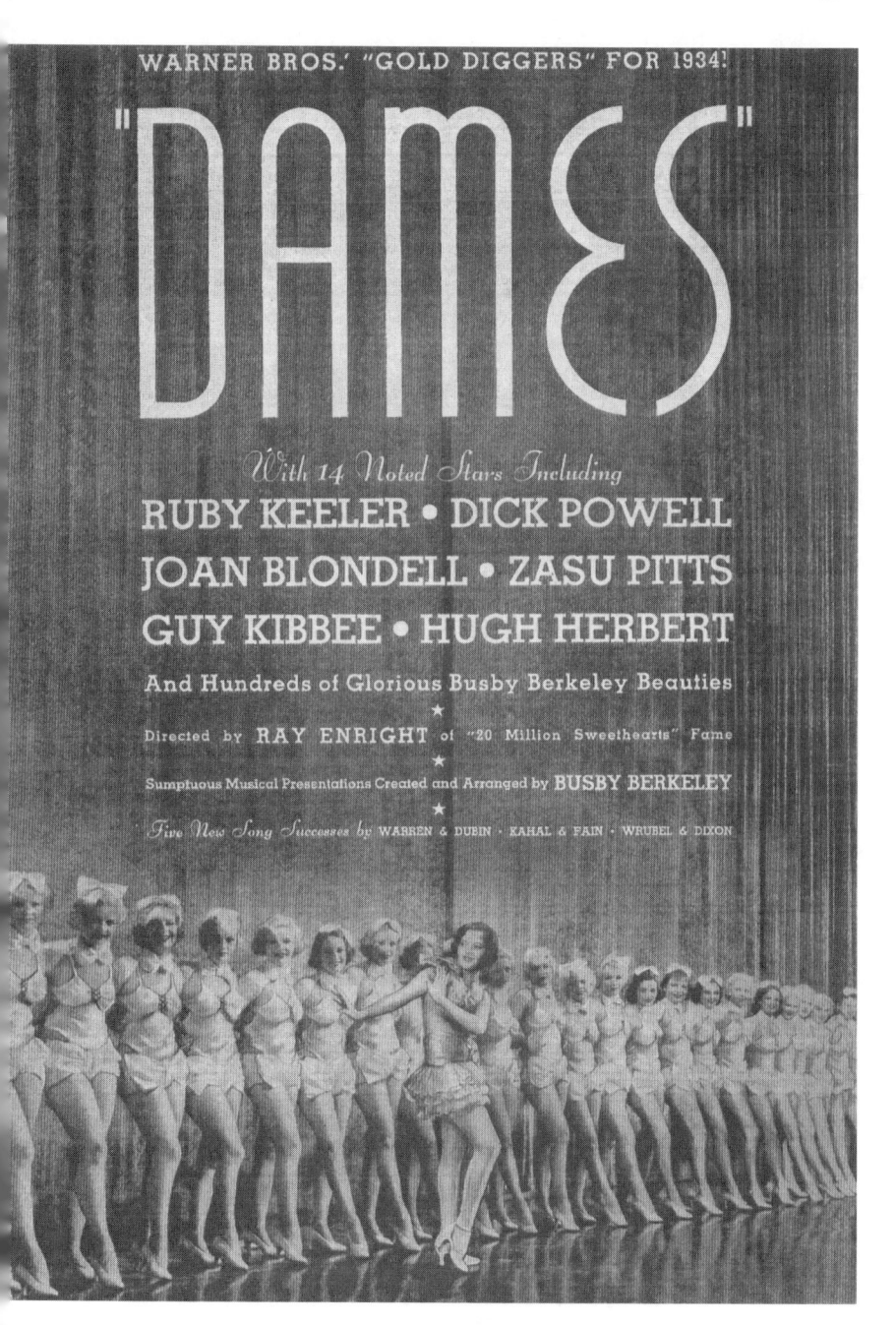

Promotional material for Dames.

MAX FACTOR COSMETICS AD, PHOTOPLAY MAGAZONE, 1934

        To quote the above advertisement: "LOVABLE CHARM— Ruby

Max Factor cosmetics ad, Photoplay Magazine, *1934. (Courtesy Max Factor.)*

Ruby on the cover of Screen Romances Magazine, *September 1934. (Courtesy of Bantam Doubleday Dell.)*

Ruby with lyricist Al Dubin, 1934. Dubin and his partner, Harry Warren, wrote the words and music for Footlight Parade, Roman Scandals, Moulin Rouge, Wonder Bar, 20 Million Sweethearts, *and* Dames. *All of this was done in ten months. The team also composed the songs for* 42nd Street *and* Golddiggers of 1933.

OPPOSITE *(Top): Henry Warren (left) and Al Dubin. Bottom: Dick Powell overburdened with Ruby's luggage in* Flirtation Walk.

(continued from page 83) discovered she was suffering from Bright's Disease (malfunction of the kidneys).

Anna May had set her heart on following in sister Ruby's footsteps, but her declining health halted all plans to start her theatrical training. A warmer climate was recommended, so Ruby and Mother Keeler took Anna May to California, where Ruby was starting to film *42nd Street*. Anna May, a lovely teenager with sparkling blue eyes became Ruby's secretary and handled all her fan mail.

Some months later, as Ruby was preparing to film *Go Into Your Dance* with Al Jolson, Anna May became seriously ill. She grew worse with each passing day, and finally, with Ruby by her bedside, she passed away at the age of 19.

Completion of her movie and plans to adopt a baby in the near future enabled Ruby to get through one of the darkest periods in her life. Al Jolson, Jr., was adopted later that year.

Go Into Your Dance

The film event of 1935 for the Jolsons was the release of their first picture together, *Go Into Your Dance*, distributed by First National. Pre-release publicity made audiences eager to see the famous couple as a husband-and-wife team. Patsy Kelly and Ruby, childhood friends, were reunited in the film. *Go Into Your Dance* had a more solid plot than the usual musical. Ruby portrayed a naive young dancer who helps actor-singer Jolson make a comeback after booze and gambling have all but ruined his career. The film also featured Glenda Farrell and Helen Morgan. Archie Mayo directed, and Bobby Connolly was the choreographer.

Keeler and Jolson played well together, and their "She's a Latin from Manhattan" number delighted their fans. Kate Cameron, *New York Daily News*, wrote, "Romantics of the picture-going world can gorge themselves as Keeler and Jolson sing, dance and make love to each other."

Shipmates Forever

Ruby was again teamed with Dick Powell in *Shipmates Forever* (1935), a successful First National release. Lacking an interesting

Powell and Keeler indulge in Flirtation Walk.

plot, the producers made do with a change in locale, moving from
Flirtation Walk's West Point to the Naval Academy at Annapolis.
Director Frank Borzage did his best with a bad script, and Ruby
again danced her way into Cadet Powell's heart.

Colleen

Sadly enough, this 1936 musical was the last film that Ruby
made with Dick Powell. Alfred E. Green directed, and Bobby

Ruby and "Cadet" Dick Powell enjoying the hula, as performed by the Sol Hoopi Native Dancers and Orchestra in Flirtation Walk.

Connolly handled the dance direction. Ruby owed Warner Bros. three pictures, so she was back under their banner.

In spite of a good cast that included Joan Blondell, Jack Oakie, Marie Wilson, Louise Fazenda, and Hugh Herbert, *Colleen* was not successful. A review in the *New York Times* called the picture "faded."

Ruby said, in an interview in 1950, "In my day, musicals didn't get any better—they just got bigger."

Ready, Willing and Able

Ray Enright directed *Ready, Willing and Able* (1937), the last film Ruby made for Warner Bros. Ruby played a would-be star who

Ruby Keeler and Dick Powell as bride and groom in a scene from Flirtation Walk.

impersonates a British actress in order to land a part in a Broadway show. Her love interest was Ross Alexander, but Ruby and her dancing partner, Lee Dixon, gave the film its top dance number. In the finale, Ruby and Dixon danced on the keys of a giant typewriter. The routine was Ruby's favorite screen dance, and she remarked (*Dance Magazine*, 1970), "I suppose you might call it one of the last of the real rhythm dance numbers. They just don't do it that way anymore." "Too Marvelous for Words" was the hit song from the pic.

The film also featured Allen Jenkins, Louise Fazenda, Carol Hughes, Ross Alexander, Wini Shaw, and Teddy Hart.

When *Ready, Willing and Able* was finished, Warners released Ruby from her contract. It was the end of the magical, musical era in films.

Mother Carey's Chickens

Ruby signed a contract with R.K.O. Pictures for two films a year at $40,000 a picture. She made only one: *Mother Carey's*

Ross Alexander and Ruby Keeler, Flirtation Walk. *Alexander was a promising young leading man in the early '30s. He appeared with Ruby in* Flirtation Walk, Shipmates Forever *and* Ready, Willing and Able. *Sadly, he committed suicide when he was only 30 years old.*

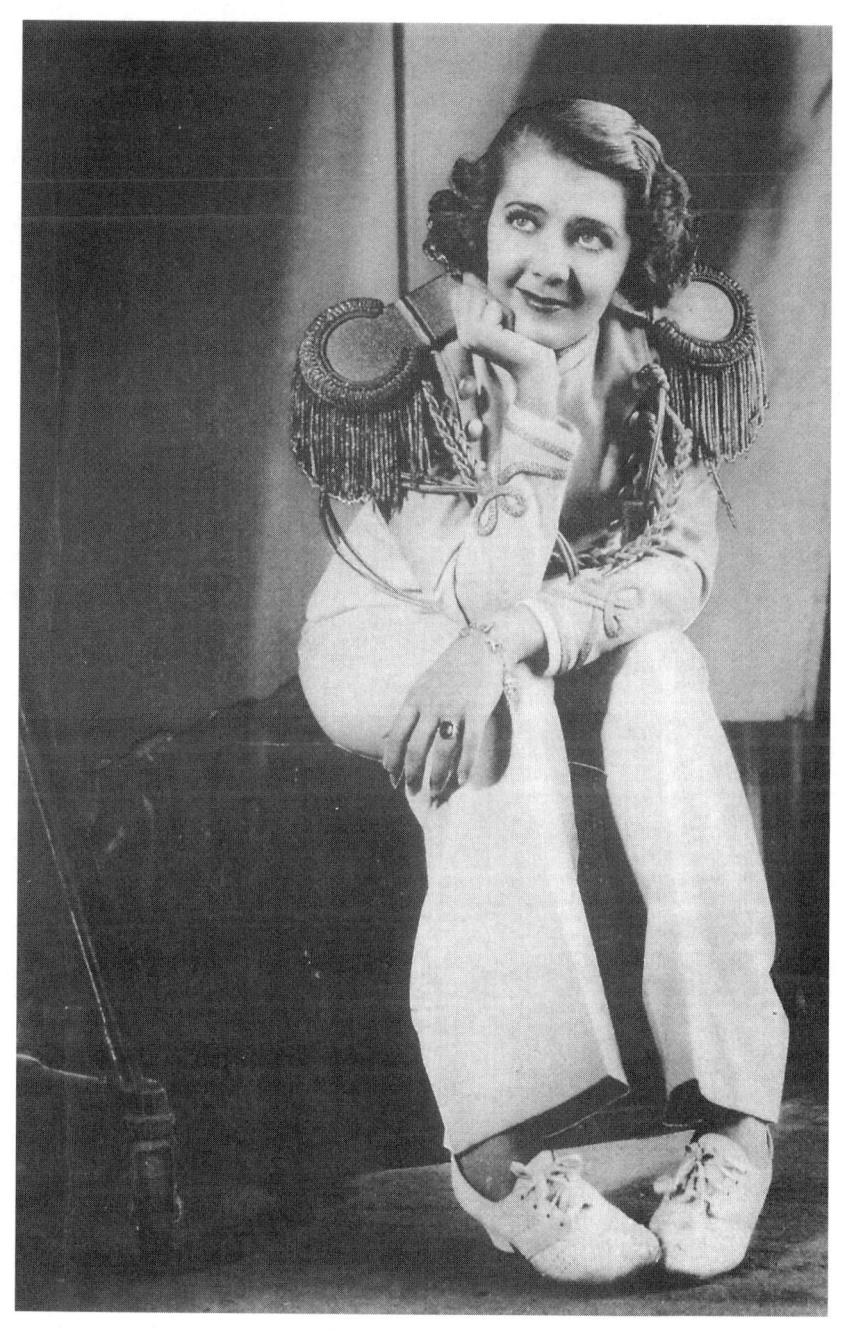

"General" Ruby Keeler, seen here in Flirtation Walk.

Ruby Keeler Jolson, Hillcrest Country Club, 1934. A little-known fact is that Ruby Keeler had great golfing ability, maintaining a ten-or-under handicap. The Jolsons belonged to the prestigious Hillcrest Country Club in Los Angeles, where Jolson had been a member for many years. He was not a golfer, but he was proud of his wife's athletic prowess and enjoyed the company of his celebrity cronies: George Burns, Jack Benny, and George Jessel. (Jessel, incidentally, turned down the lead in The Jazz Singer *and always regretted it.)*

OPPOSITE *(Top):* Movie Mirror, *July 1935: Anna May Keeler pictured with sister Ruby. Bottom: Ruby (with her mother, Elnora Keeler) holds baby Al Jolson, Jr., adopted in 1935.*

Ruby
Keeler

MEETS
SORROW

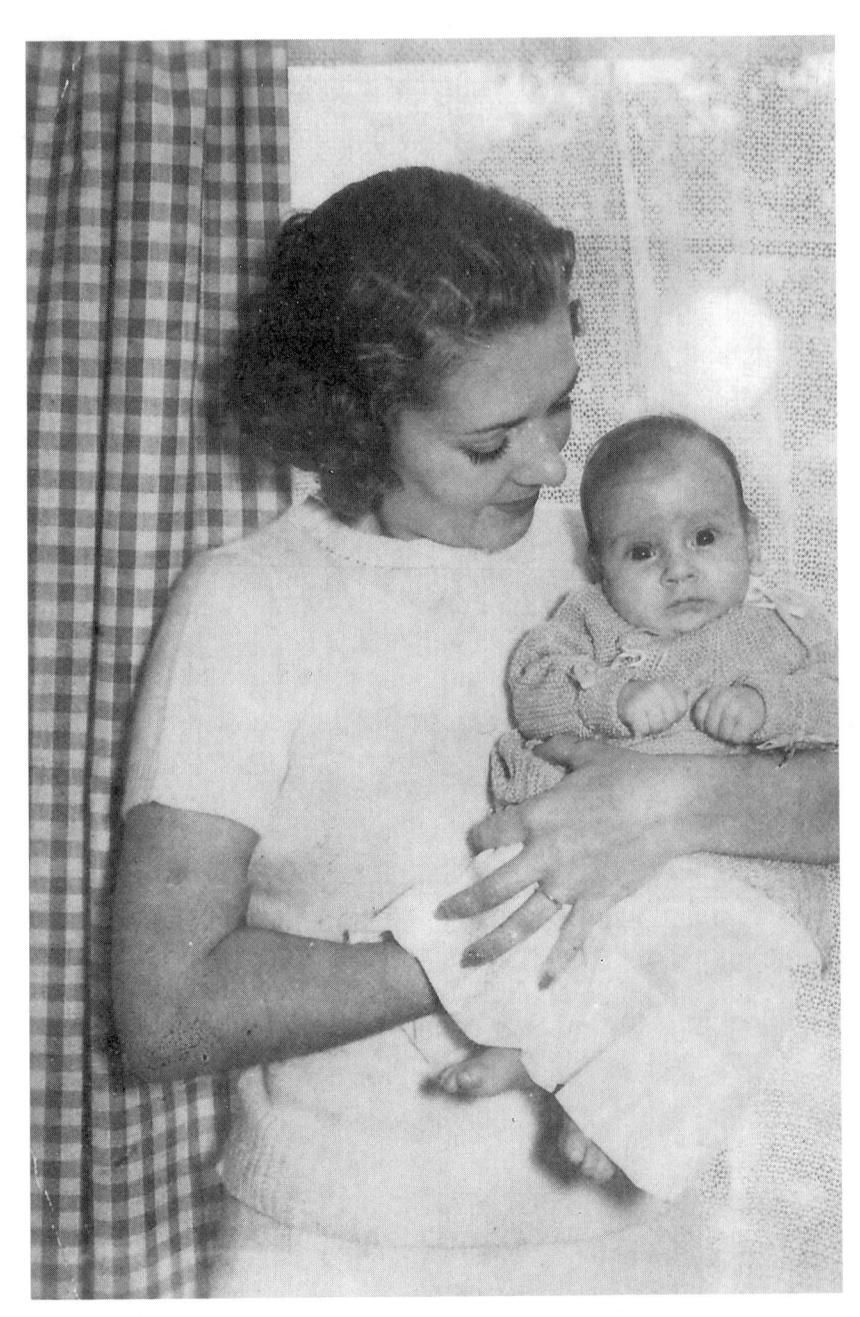

Ruby and baby Al Jr. at home in the Talmadge apartments on Wilshire Boulevard, Los Angeles.

Ruby in full dress with two members of the chorus for the film Go Into Your
Dance.

Mr. and Mrs. Al Jolson featured on the sheet music for their hit musical number, "About a Quarter to Nine."

OPPOSITE: Ruby is "A Latin from Manhattan" in this musical number from Go Into Your Dance. In this lavish production, Ruby pretends she is Senorita Donnalu—A sensation from South America.

Publicity for Go Into Your Dance.

First exclusive showing of the new Keeler in *Shipmates Forever*

Photographed at Warner Brothers Studio by Bert Longworth

Bert Longworth photographed Ruby performing some tap dancing steps at Warner Bros. Studios during the filming of Shipmates Forever. *This particular step was actually called the "sea twist."*

OPPOSITE: Shipmates Forever.

(continued from page 93) Chickens (1938). In the billing, Ruby was listed below Anne Shirley, and she terminated her contract with R.K.O. Keeler's role was originally offered to Katharine Hepburn. Hepburn refused to do the part and bought her way out of her contract for $220,000.

Mother Carey's Chickens was Ruby's only film without music. It was a departure from the lavish musicals that had made her a star and was her only straight dramatic role.

Ruby Keeler's marriage to Al Jolson ended in 1939. Madelyn Fio-Rito Jones, one of Ruby's closest friends, told the author what she remembered about the breakup.

Ruby with Al Jr. on Christmas Eve 1936. (AP/Wide World Photos.)

"One night," she said, "after a card game, our mutual friend, comedian Bert Wheeler, drove Ruby home to her Encino, California, ranch. Jolson was doing his radio show in Hollywood but happened to arrive home at the same time." Ruby was giving Wheeler a thank-you kiss on the cheek when Jolson arrived. "It was

Dick Powell and Ruby Keeler in their last teaming, the 1936 film Colleen.

dark, so all he could see was his wife kissing some man's cheek," Jones continued.

Jones said Jolson was furious and put Ruby through the "third degree"—who was she kissing, why was she so late, and on and on with his usual jealous tirade. "Ruby never gave Al any reason not to trust her," Jones said. "She was the most loyal human being in the

THIS PAGE AND OPPOSITE TOP: *Two photos of Ruby Keeler and Al Jolson in 1936.*
OPPOSITE BOTTOM: *Palm Springs, California, February 10, 1936. Ruby Keeler
Jolson relaxing poolside with her mother and sisters at the El Mirador Hotel, a
favorite retreat for the rich and famous in the 1930s. Left to right: Margie, Ruby,
Gertrude, and Elnora.*

world and strictly a family person. I never heard her say an unkind
word about anybody."

Jones went on: "Ruby called me the next morning and said
she'd had it. She said she had to get away from Al's jealousy and
possessiveness. The very next day, she hired an attorney and started
divorce proceedings."

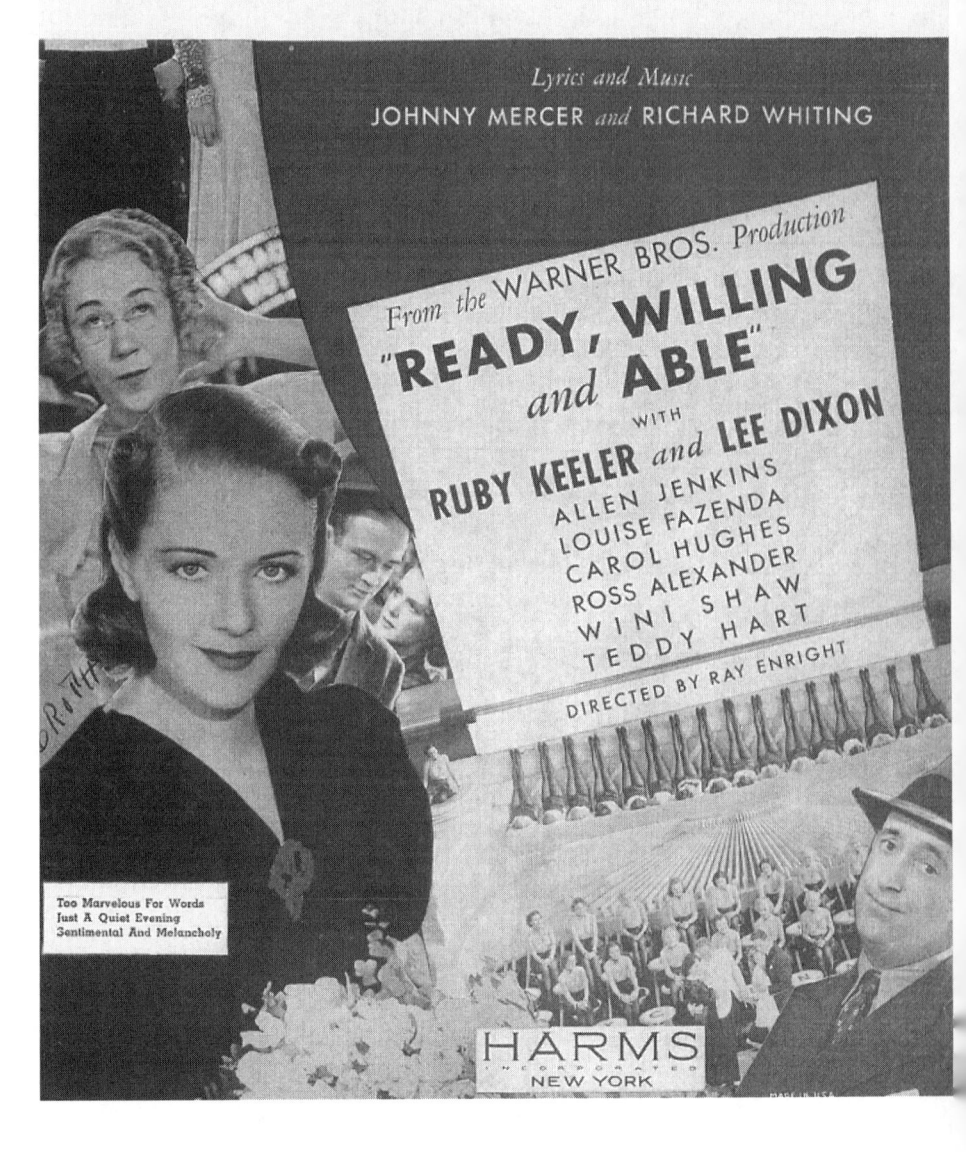

Sheet music for "Too Marvelous for Words," the hit song from Ready, Willing and Able.

Ruby dancing with Lee Dixon in Ready, Willing and Able, *released March 16, 1937.*

By that time the domestic problems of the Jolsons were common knowledge. The conflict in their careers had always put a strain on the marriage, but above all, the differences in their personalities, ages, religions, and tastes proved insurmountable.

Despite her stardom, Ruby was basically a very shy lady who disliked crowds and large parties. In 1938, she had gone to Honolulu alone, and the public knew at that time that the marriage was in serious trouble. When Ruby returned from Hawaii, she

Ruby as she appeared in Ready, Willing and Able.

agreed to appear with her husband in a play called *Hold On to Your Hat*. She walked out of it in Chicago when Jolson kept making references to their marital problems during rehearsals.

In October 1939, Ruby's lawyer announced the Jolsons had separated. Jolson told the press, "Our family troubles are not important enough to bring about a divorce." Nevertheless, on December 26, 1939, an interlocutory decree was handed down, with

Ruby in Ready, Willing and Able.

Ruby alleging mental cruelty. She said at the time, "Al never agreed with me on anything and called me stupid in public." Jolson, in turn, said, "Ruby's a wonderful girl, and I'm sorry if I've given her an inferiority complex. I hope we reconcile."

The divorce became final a year later, and Ruby told the press her marriage to Jolson was "a mistake—a long mistake."

ABOVE: *Ruby Keeler Jolson with younger sister Helen in New York, 1938.*
OPPOSITE *(Top): Martha Raye (left), clowning it up with Ruby Keeler Jolson and Gertrude Keeler in New York, 1937. Raye was a comedienne and vocalist whose career spanned almost 40 years in motion pictures and television. Bottom: Ruby and Al showing the big city to Margie Keeler.*

Ruby and Al Jolson relaxing in the den of their ranch in Encino, California, 1938.

Ruby and her son, Al Jr., poolside (1938).

Ruby in Los Angeles court, December 26, 1939. She was granted a divorce from Al Jolson, alleging mental cruelty (AP/Wide World Photos).

Ruby Keeler and Al Jolson, New York, 1938. As always, Jolson was very aware of the camera as he kissed his wife's cheek.

CHAPTER 3

Mr. and Mrs. John Lowe and Family, 1941–1969

Since playing golf was one of the great loves of Ruby's life, it was only natural that she would meet her future husband at a golf club. While having dinner with friends, Ruby was introduced to handsome bachelor John Homer Lowe. It was love at first sight, even though Margie Keeler-Weatherwax says that Ruby first tried to fix Lowe up with sister Gertrude.

Ruby and Lowe were completely compatible. They shared the same hopes and dreams for their future—to settle down and raise a family. Ruby had retired from show business, and Lowe was already established as a prominent California real estate broker and builder. On October 29, 1941, the marriage took place at St. Charles Borremeo Church in North Hollywood, California.

Ruby said, "Once I became Mrs. John Lowe, it never entered my head to be or do anything else. I enjoyed my career, but I always knew there was more to life than making movies." (Article in *Films in Review* by Ronald L. Bowers.)

The Lowes lived a very private life, residing in Orange County for most of their marriage. Madelyn Fio-Rito Jones told the author, "Because Al Jolson had given Ruby an inferiority complex, especially about having their own children, Ruby was terribly worried about this issue in her new life with Lowe." Jones said Ruby told her husband of this fear, and he said, "I don't care about anything but you, Ruby. I love *you*." A year and a half later, their first daughter, Theresa, was born. Ruby said on this joyous occasion, "Having this baby was up to the Lord." Christine, John, Jr., and Kathleen arrived in the ensuing years. Ruby and Jolson's adopted son, Al Jr., grew up with the Lowe family. Ruby said in a later interview, "My life was rewarding, exciting, and fulfilling. I carted the children to school, athletic events, parties, proms, and graduation ceremonies. I can't begin to tell you how wonderful it was."

In between, Ruby always made time to enjoy her favorite sport—golf. She was an excellent golfer with a ten handicap. The Lowes joined Lakeside Golf Club in Toluca Lake, California, in 1941. Besides her duties as a caring wife and mother, Ruby found time to improve her game on the Lakeside links. Lakeside was

PREVIOUS PAGE: Lt. and Mrs. John Lowe, with Al Jolson, Jr., in Toluca Lake, California, 1941.

OPPOSITE *(Top): Ruby and John Lowe with Mrs. Elnora Keeler, 1941. Bottom: Ruby and John with baby Theresa, 1943.*

Ruby with her "stepping stones": Theresa, Christine, and John Lowe, Jr.

Baby Christine Lowe with mother and older sister, Theresa, 1945.

famous in its own right, having a long list of prestigious celebrities
on its membership roster. That list included Bing Crosby, Bob
Hope, Oliver Hardy, W.C. Fields, Howard Hughes, and Johnny
Weismuller, to name just a few.

Ruby played in Dolores Hope's "Hope-ful Tournament" with

The Lowes with Al Jr., 1945.

her friends and one year competed in the Women's State Championship, along with Hope. Her dear friend and golfing pal Mary Hanneberg, told the author recently from her home in Palm Springs, California, "My golfing friends at Lakeside were all excellent golfers, including my Ruby. I met her at Lakeside in 1941 when she was engaged to John Lowe. They really enjoyed playing golf together."

Ruby would appear in only two more films, with nearly 30 years passing between the two. On June 30, 1941, Columbia released *Sweetheart of the Campus,* featuring Ruby as a cynical, wise-cracking showgirl. (This bit of miscasting may have been one reason for the picture's lack of success.) The picture also featured bandleader Ozzie Nelson and his orchestra along with Nelson's future wife, Harriet Hilliard. Edward Dmytryk directed, and the cast included Gordon Oliver, Don Beddoe, and Kathleen Howard.

ABOVE AND OPPOSITE: *Three scenes from* Sweetheart of the Campus.

Ruby's final film appearance was in a 1970 bomb called *The Phynx*. Cinematically incompetent, it was released into very few theatres and then withdrawn completely. *The Phynx* was an absurd story about a rock group trying to rescue film stars from a foreign country behind the iron curtain. Perhaps in his own attempt at rescue, director Lee Katzin filled the film to the brim with stars doing cameo bits. The presence of Ruby, Busby Berkeley, Joan Blondell, Patsy Kelly, Edgar Bergen and Charlie McCarthy, Dorothy Lamour, Martha Raye, Ed Sullivan, and others never helped to resuscitate *The Phynx*.

Hanneberg related her favorite golf story: "I was playing eighteen with Ruby at Lakeside one day, and she was annoyed with herself because she thought she was swaying, not turning. What did that dear girl do? She took a swing and purposely took a playful bite out of her own arm to prove she had turned!"

Hanneberg wistfully said, "Ruby was always a joy to be with. She was a dear, dear friend; and to this day, I miss her terribly."

Ruby's dancing talent was also used at Lakeside. This author was among those who wrote, directed and danced in the ladies' golf shows, which were put on for the Women's Invitational Tournament

Nancy Marlow-Trump (left) appraising Ruby Keeler's "swing." Lakeside Golf Club, Burbank, California, June 1954.

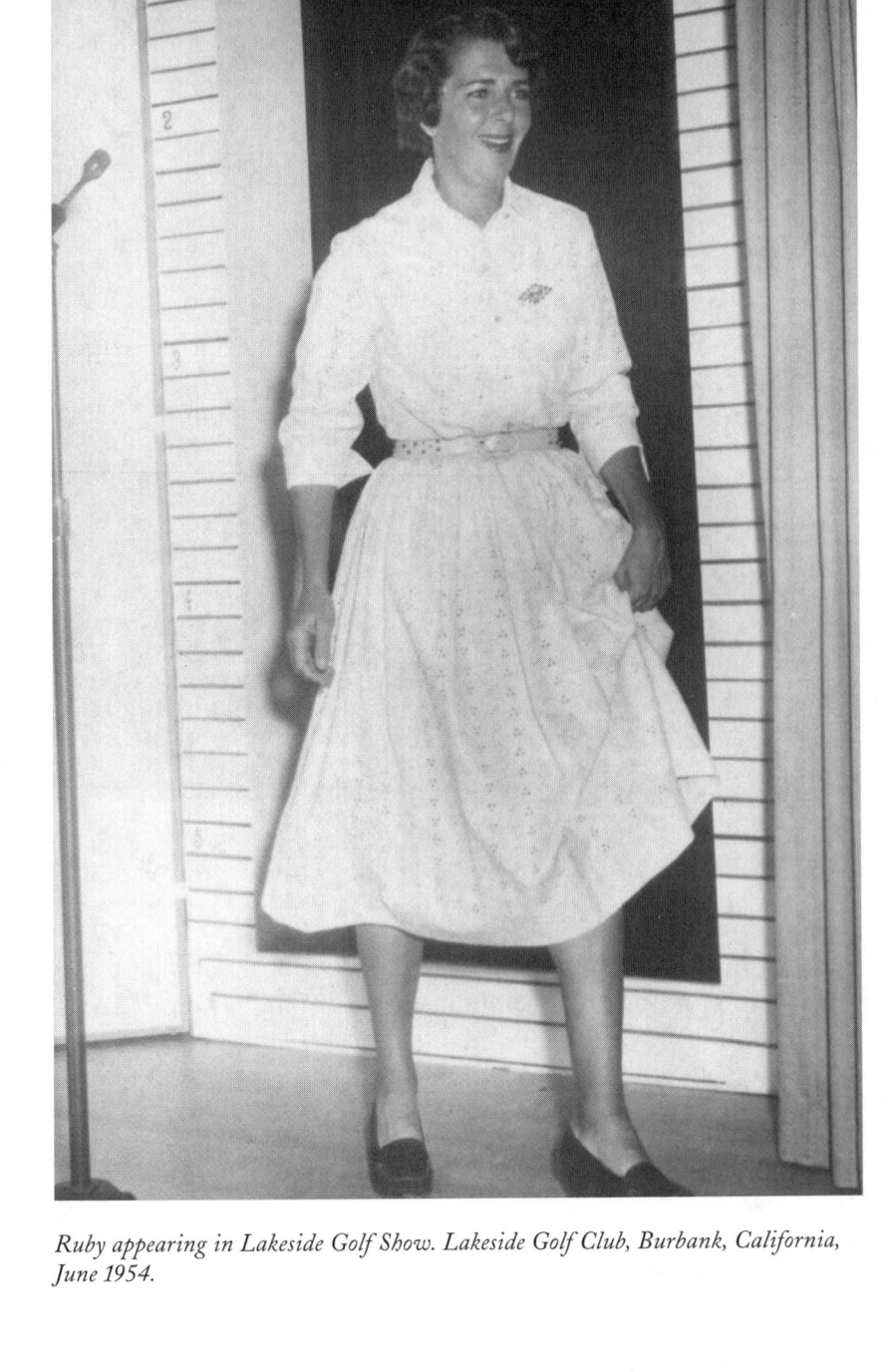

Ruby appearing in Lakeside Golf Show. Lakeside Golf Club, Burbank, California,
June 1954.

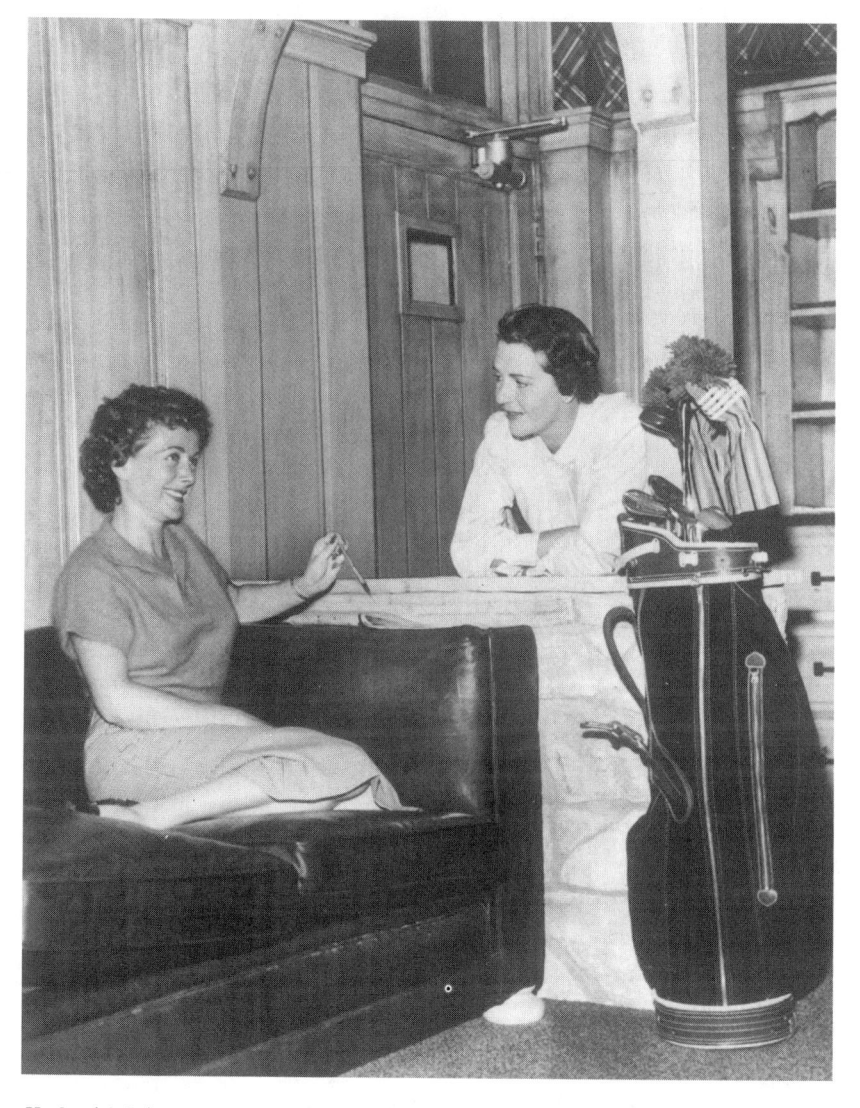

Keeler (right) and Marlow-Trump discussing golf scores. Lakeside Golf Club, Burbank, California, June 1954.

once a year. In the late '40s, '50s, and '60s, the cast in the shows read like a top Broadway show. There was comedienne Cass Daley, Dolores (Mrs. Bob) Hope, Sheila (Mrs. Gordon) MacRae, Addie (Mrs. Jimmy) Fidler, Marilyn (Mrs. Forrest) Tucker, Frances (Mrs. Neal) Hefti and Elsie (Mrs. Andy) Clyde. What a thrill it was for

Ruby Keeler with her daughters in 1970. From left to right: Theresa, Ruby,
Christine, and Kathleen Lowe.

this author to be "directing" Ruby Keeler.

In a recent interview with the author, Ruby's son, John Lowe,
Jr., stressed that the main interest in her life was being a mother.
"Mom was always the driver when I was in grammar school," Lowe
said. "She participated in all our school activities and was always
there for us. I'll never forget how caring she was."

In a letter to the author dated June 1996, Theresa Hall Lowe
wrote lovingly of her mother, Ruby Keeler Lowe:

> Memories of Mom begin with and continue to be love and
> devotion to her family and her Catholic faith. She was
> unwavering in both. Both Mom and Dad encouraged us in any
> pursuit in which we had an interest, and Mom was the one who
> drove us to every event. She would cheer loudly and
> distinctively so we would be able to hear her.
>
> Today, I'm involved in athletics from a coaching standpoint;
> and I draw inspiration from my Mom—dancer, golfer and
> ardent fan. Her spirit of fun, her unselfishness, her sense of

sportsmanship and commitment to excellence have provided a model from which I derive the strength, energy and enthusiasm to be the best person I can be.

Theresa's letter continued:

> Mom touched the lives of all who met her. In striving toward that goal for myself, her example is always paramount in my mind. To the Lowe children, Ruby Keeler was never a star. She was a Mom, just like everyone else's Mom ... except our Mom danced in the kitchen.

CHAPTER 4

No, No, Nanette,
1971–1973

In its first run, *No, No, Nanette* was one of the most long-delayed and eagerly anticipated shows ever to come to Broadway. It opened in 1925, but had been promised a year earlier. Its writers, Irving Caesar, Otto Harbach and Frank Mandel were the top librettists and lyricists of the time; composer Vincent Youmans was also at the top of his field. Well-loved actors and actresses were in the cast. It had opened in Chicago, but it took more than a year to arrive on Broadway. This made expectations of its arrival even more tantalizing.

Every month the producer would announce a New York opening date and then postpone it. Actually, business was so good in Chicago, the producer hated to end the run. In the meantime, four roadshows were taking *Nanette* across the country. There was even a company in London—but not New York. Gossip had it that the Shuberts would build two more theatres before *Nanette* ever got to town.

The delay was due to producer H.H. Frazee's nervousness about opening on the Great White Way. Frazee was a diligent, astute showman who, at the time, owned the Boston Red Sox. He had also just sold the world-famous Babe Ruth to the New York Yankees for a very large sum of money.

Nanette had originally opened in Detroit and had received bad press. It was also shunned in Cincinnati. Composer Youmans and writers and Mandel wanted to close the show and rewrite it. Frazee said no and opened in Chicago. The show, as it was, bombed once again.

Despite heavy losses, Frazee persisted. He got new songs, a new director, and a new cast. This time around, the audience and critics loved the show and praised it wholeheartedly. Delighted, Frazee paraphrased *Henry IV*: "Out of this nettle, defeat, we pluck this flower, a hit."

In spite of the Chicago success, he stalled for eleven more months. When *Nanette* finally opened on Broadway, the public was elated and showed their delight by dancing on the streets.

Irving Caesar, co-author with Otto Harback of the song lyrics, said many years later at the opening of the 1971 revival, *No No, Nanette* has been playing somewhere ever since it opened in 1924."

PREVIOUS PAGE: *Stage manager John Lowe, Jr., with his mother, Ruby Keeler— backstage,* No, No, Nanette, *1971.*

Program for the 1971 revival of No, No, Nanette *billed the show as "the New 1925 Musical."*

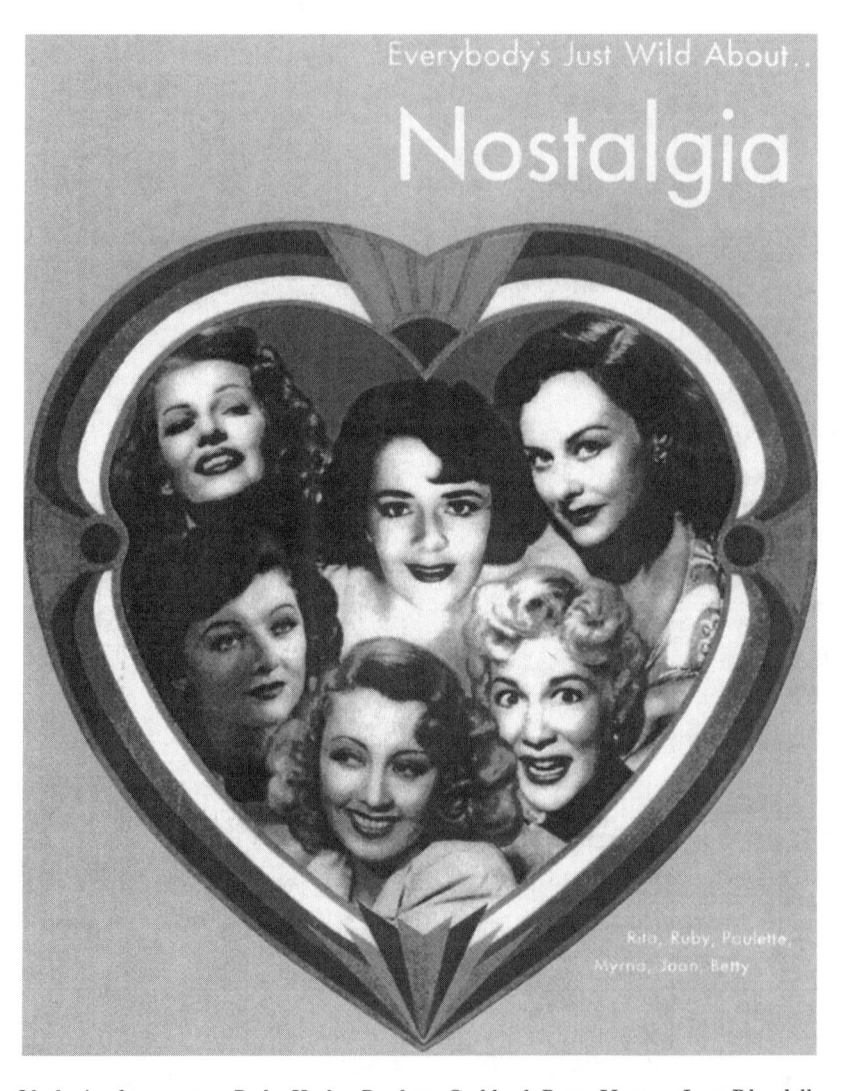

Clockwise from center: Ruby Keeler, Paulette Goddard, Betty Hutton, Joan Blondell, Myrna Loy, Rita Hayworth. From Life, *February 19, 1971. (Used by permission.)*

At that time, Caesar was the only surviving member of the original *Nanette* team.

Vincent Youmans was one of the foremost composers of stage music of his day. He wrote the score for the first Fred Astaire-Ginger Rogers film musical *Flying Down to Rio.* Yet none of his great hit songs ever matched the success of *Nanette's* "Tea for Two."

NOSTALGIA

♥ NO, NO, NANETTE
♥ BUSBY BERKELEY

ld is in, and we are happily awash in the sleek and gaudy period that stretched from the '20s through the '30s and into the '40s. Ruby Keeler, seen above as she was in 1934, returns triumphantly to Broadway, and tap dancers start warming up all over town.

Life, *February 19, 1971.*

Otto Harbach, co-author of *Nanette,* was one of the most prolific writers for the stage in the twentieth century. Frank Mandel, who along with Harbach wrote the book of *Nanette,* co-produced such major hits as "The Desert Song" and "New Moon" with Oscar Hammerstein. Harbach died in 1963 at age 89, and Mandel passed away in Hollywood in 1958, age 74.

In 1971, *No, No, Nanette* came back to Broadway in a hugely successful revival—with Ruby Keeler in the cast. It opened to rave reviews on January 19. Strangely enough, it played at the 46th Street Theatre ... and it had been 46 years since *Nanette* had originally opened on Broadway! Coincidence? Maybe...

This time around, the show was adapted and directed by Burt Shevelove and choreographed by Donald Sadler. Costumes were designed by Raoul du Bois, and both Sadler and du Bois won Tony awards for the excellence of their contributions to the show. Featured with Ruby were dancer Bobby Van, Helen Gallagher, Benny Baker, and Ruby's old friend comedienne Patsy Kelly. The production was supervised by another dear old friend of Ruby's— Busby Berkeley.

Nanette became one of the biggest musical hits to capture New York in over a decade. Some $35,000 worth of tickets were sold on the day the first reviews came out, and block-long lines formed at the box office. The lines were still there 25 months later, and the nostalgia craze had hit New York with an "I Want to Be Happy" bang. *Life Magazine* devoted a special half-issue to the sudden yearning for the glamorous past.

The show ran to packed houses through February 3, 1973, for a total of 861 performances. Three touring companies set out across the United States, and everywhere, *Nanette* was greeted with cheering, enchanted audiences. Ruby Keeler had not only captivated her old fans, but won the hearts of thousands of new ones.

Various factors influenced Ruby to do the show. Her husband, John Lowe, had passed away in early 1969, sadly ending their very happy 27-year marriage. Her five children were grown and on their own. Her friends and children urged her to do the show. This author, in fact, played a tiny part in the urging when she visited Ruby in Newport Beach in 1970. "What do you think, Nancy, shall I do it?" Ruby asked. Without a moment's hesitation, the author answered: "Yes! The timing is right, and you'll be terrific." Easy to guess those beautiful blue eyes and talented dancing feet couldn't miss.

Ruby went on to explain that she had gotten a call from producer Harry Rigby. "Rigby asked me if I wanted to do a Broadway show," she said. "I didn't know him, and I was flabbergasted." She added, with eyes twinkling, "I haven't exactly kept up with anyone on Broadway these days. Getting back into show business was the furthest thing from my mind."

Ruby, however, was encouraged to read the script of *No, No, Nanette* and was certainly pleased that her friend Busby Berkeley would supervise the show. She liked the part and knew she could still dance. In an interview for *Dance Magazine* (December 1970), Ruby said, "If I do the show, I'm going to wander around the East Side looking for the landmarks of my early years. I loved the fire escape of an old apartment we lived in. I'm going to find it."

Ruby accepted the challenge, and her return to Broadway was, in fact, a phenomenon. The 60-year-old show biz veteran made what newsman John Schubeck of WABC-TV (New York) called "the entertainment comeback of the century." Golf and swimming had kept Ruby in excellent physical condition, and the beautiful blue-eyed grandmother certainly had not forgotten her tap-dancing skills. Her family provided her with a built-in security blanket, standing by her, working with her, and praying for her success. Son John Lowe, Jr., accompanied his mother to New York and was assistant stage manager for *Nanette*. Sister Gertrude was Ruby's personal secretary and dresser.

In an interview, John Jr. told the author, "I thought the show would be good for her. It would be fun, and the whole family thought it was a great idea." He added, "At first, I got involved as Mom's 'protector.' Rigby really wanted her for the show and asked me if I would come with her as stage manager. I'm so grateful we had the *Nanette* years together. Mom was terrific. She had a renewed interest in life and never played the 'star.' What I remember in particular was the way Mom handled herself. She was pretty great."

Lowe continued to reminisce: "I remember the sense of accomplishment I felt and how wonderful that time was. For me especially, it was the beginning of a new career and a new life. I also had a deep appreciation of Mom and a fine relationship with her. *Nanette* helped her get over her sadness at losing Dad. She was surrounded by very close friends; Patsy was in the show, and her sister Gertrude was right there to help. It seemed to me that everyone knew her, and she knew everybody. The pros in the show adored her." Lowe said proudly, "I don't think there was a person alive that didn't love my mother."

Lowe said he thought the magic of *Nanette* worked because his mother and the cast had special feelings for each other. "That aura around us can never be duplicated," Lowe said. "Mom certainly had a new lifestyle and new pressures, but she wore it well. She still played her golf, went shopping, and of course, always had time for her family and friends."

Ruby said of her comeback (*Dance Magazine*, 1970), "I was very lucky. Too many people try to keep the image they once had on screen. I was too busy being a wife and mother. It really made the transition easy for me."

On May 14, 1971, Ruby was awarded the George M. Cohan Award by the Catholic Actors' Guild. It was a moving tribute, since it was a Cohan production that first brought her to the Broadway stage.

Critics unanimously agreed that Ruby *was* the show—she made it work. Richard Phillips observed in *After Dark Magazine* (March 1971), "She doesn't miss a trick, dancing across that stage, her brows knit with merriment and concentration and her mouth in a wide O of wonder. It's as if she was saying, 'It's really me, and the gang's all here for a nifty fun fest.'" Perhaps Ruby herself knew the timing was perfect and this was her moment to enjoy the spotlight once again. She told the press in a 1971 interview, "This going back to Broadway is a one time thing. I'm going for a 'visit,' and that's all. I'm a family person, and I can't stay away from them too long."

When Ruby decided to go on tour with *No, No, Nanette*, the singing actor Don Ameche was the perfect choice to hit the road with her. Keeler and Ameche were emblems of an era of quality entertainment—distinguished professionals.

Ameche, probably best remembered for his starring role in *Alexander Graham Bell*, had a long line of Broadway, radio, television, and screen credits.

John Dwyer (*Buffalo Evening News*, June 1974) said of this unique pair, "The audience reaction was interesting. With Don Ameche, it was genuine warmth and affection. With Ruby Keeler, it was love, love, love."

Dwyer added, "The show, 'No, No, Nanette,' is cheery and appealing, but it revolves around the heart-lifting sight of Ruby Keeler dancing rings around her show-business grandchildren, tearing up the calendar and throwing it in the face of time."

CHAPTER 5

The Twilight Years, 1974–1993

John Lowe, Jr., described the tragedy that struck his lovely mother in 1974: "I was on the road with *No, No, Nanette* when I received the phone call from my sister Christine. Mom had had an aneurysm while visiting her grandchildren in Montana and was unconscious. We were all completely stunned.

My sisters and I pulled together to walk through this nightmare with Mom. We had to decide what we should and shouldn't do immediately. Was Great Falls, Montana, 125 miles away by ambulance, the right place to take her? How good were the doctors there? There were too many questions and no answers.

We learned a great deal in a shot amount of time. She went through brain surgery, which was very dangerous at that point, and none of us knew if she would survive. She was given physical therapy, also, and that was very painful for her.

Mom floated in and out of consciousness, remembering certain instances in her life. They weren't sad things—just incidents that came into her mind at the time. Mainly, she remembered being in Hawaii....

When she was able to go home to Newport Beach, California, my sister Kathleen left her job in New York to live with Mom. I always felt that once she recovered from surgery, she was going to be whole again. I knew she'd have physical problems; but I had no doubt in my mind, none of us did, that Mom would be completely well again. Thank God, we were right," Lowe said.

Ruby's tremendous faith in God and her strength and courage pulled her through the greatest challenge in her life. The blue eyes never lost their sparkle, and she was determined to be well again. After two months in the hospital, she returned to her home in Newport Beach, where she began strenuous physical therapy.

When the family thought Ruby was well enough, they decided to book a voyage on the cruise ship *Rotterdam*. Kathleen would accompany her mother on this all-important step toward recovery. It was 1979—five years after the aneurysm.

Destiny works in miraculous ways. Ruby was immediately recognized by two English entertainers on board ship—Jackie and Roy Toaduff. They had seen Ruby's brilliant comeback in *No, No, Nanette* in 1972. Jackie Toaduff had been introduced to her

PREVIOUS PAGE: *Ruby Keeler in Rancho Mirage, California, 1992.*

CRUISE DIRECTOR: BOB HAINES

AT SEA—WEDNESDAY 6 MAY 1981

At 9.30 p.m.
Dancing and Entertainment with
FOUR OF A KIND
and the
RONNIE CARYL ORCHESTRA

At 10.30 p.m.—SHOWTIME
presenting
ROY & JACKIE TOADUFF
IN
"HELLO BROADWAY"
with the
IRVING DAVIES DANCERS
and
THE RONNIE CARYL ORCHESTRA

RUBY KEELER

AT 2.45 P.M. IN THE THEATRE

••

The Leisure Office, situated on Upper Deck in
the Theatre Bar (near 'E' Elevator), is open
today from 10.00 a.m. to Noon and from 2.30
p.m. to 5.00 p.m.

••

ROY & JACKIE TOADUFF

● At 2.45 p.m. in the Theatre ●
"FROM FORTY-SECOND STREET TO THE QUEEN ELIZABETH 2"
JACKIE TOADUFF
interviews
RUBY KEELER

Program from Ruby's appearance on the cruise ship Queen Elizabeth 2.

backstage at the 46th Street Theatre in New York and again at
Sardi's Restaurant.

Toaduff told the author on her recent visit to England, "I saw
this lady in the distance accompanied by a lovely young woman. She
was handicapped and walking with a cane, but her beautiful blue
eyes hadn't changed. I knew it was Ruby Keeler."

After once again meeting Ruby and daughter Kathleen, the

Toaduffs asked her to join them for their evening performance on ship. Ruby was delighted and said, "I'd be thrilled to attend."

No passenger was aware Ruby was aboard the *Rotterdam.* That evening, the Toaduffs decided to do a salute to her in the dining salon. After a royal introduction, Ruby stood up and waved. Everyone gasped, and then the wild applause began. The audience then arose en masse and gave Ruby a standing ovation. "It was exactly like an opening night on Broadway," Toaduff said. "Ruby cried, her daughter cried; and tears were flowing in the orchestra and in the audience." After the show, Ruby's daughter told the Toaduffs, "You've done so much for my mother and made her very happy. Thank you."

Jackie and Roy Toaduff, international entertainers, and their manager, Colin Edwards, were responsible for starting a new career for Ruby. They introduced her to the world of celebrity cruises by having the Cunard Line book her onto the QE, *Queen Elizabeth 2,* where they had entertained for 20 years. Toaduff said, "We feel we gave Ruby a new lease on life. She had to have a purpose and to feel 'wanted' once again." He added, "We traveled the world together, and Ruby regained her confidence. Whenever she appeared, the audience would always give her a standing ovation."

Ruby often visited her friends Jackie and Roy Toaduff, who owned the Chantry Hotel in Dronfield, England. All in all, she made six trips to the beautiful Derbyshire countryside. She would also phone the Toaduffs at least once a week just to stay in touch. The *Sheffield Star* quoted Ruby on October 11, 1982, as saying, "I'd like to stay here forever. It reminds me of my homeland in Nova Scotia, Canada."

Nevertheless, it was to Rancho Mirage, California, that Ruby moved in the early 1980s. The desert climate and a score of friends helped her even more on the road to recovery. She became active in the Stroke Activity Center in Palm Desert. Dr. Irving Hirshleifer, founder and president of the board, said (*The Desert Sun,* 1984), "Ms. Keeler gets 'strokers' up and out of their wheelchairs to dance with her when she visits the center." Ruby's advice to all of them was, "Continue to do as much as you possibly can. Use the facilities you have, and live life to its fullest."

Ruby made many local appearances and was honored by the Desert Theatre League, the Palm Springs International Film

DAILY *VARIETY*

85 CENTS
MONDAY
MARCH 1, 1993

A CANNERS PUBLICATION • LOS ANGELES, CALIFORNIA • NEWSPAPER SECOND CLASS P.O. ENTRY

LEGENDARY KEELER DIES OF CANCER AT 83

BY RICHARD NATALE

Ruby Keeler, stage and screen actress whose name became inextricably linked with the Depression era musicals of choreographer/director Busby Berkeley, ~~~ester-day of cancer at her ~~~ cho Mirage. She w~~~

Though her car~~~ handful of Broadway ~~~usical films, Keeler ep~~~ ~~~orking chorine loc~~~ ~~he back line ~~~

vote herself to married life, first to the legendary Al Jolson and subsequently to real estate broker John Homer Lowe.

"I couldn't have cared less about having a career," Keeler once said. "I always felt there was more to life than showbiz. The idea of early retirement appealed to me no end."

Born Aug. 25, 1909, in Halifax, ~~va Scotia, Keeler was raised in ~~rk. After studying dance as a ~~ied her way into the cho-~~ but said she was 16) ~~n's "The Rise of ~~~ ~~tonished

Ruby Keeler in "Dames" (193

She received good notic her next show, the 1927 n "Bye Bye Bonnie" in which s ~~~ "Tampico Tap." "I

Musicals star Ruby Keeler of '42nd St.' dies

(AP) — Ruby Keeler, the win-some dancer who tapped her way through a string of glittering Warner Bros. musicals in the 1930s, died Sunday at her Southern California desert home. She was 83.

Keeler died of cancer in Rancho Mirage, 110 miles east of Los An-
~~~ John Lowe.

Ruby Keeler: A Cheerfully Optimistic Trouper Bidding Farewell to

THE HOLLYWOOD REPORTER

Monday, March 1, 1993

95¢ *(California)* $1.50 *(Elsewhere)*

Copyright 199--Variety, Inc.
Reprinted With Permission

TRIBUTE

A PASSING OF LEGENDS
Death claims a pair of originals,
Lillian Gish and Ruby Keeler

Collage of headlines announcing Ruby Keeler's death. (Variety masthead and article and Hollywood Reporter masthead reprinted with permission.)

Festival, and the Palm Springs Performing Arts Center. A shining star was placed in front of the Plaza Theatre in her honor.

The late columnist Frederick Heider (*Desert Sun*, 1988), wrote: "Legendary singing-dancing star, Ruby Keeler, was seen at the Desert Dixieland Festival. When the musicians heard she was there, they sent her an invitation to join them. When Ruby arrived, she put aside her cane, asked the band to play one of 'her' songs and began to dance. The old Keeler magic went into action as she kicked up a storm of nostalgia to a wild, standing ovation."

Among Ruby's many friends in the desert were Sam Robson and Joe Burns. When interviewed at their Palm Springs home, Burns said Ruby nicknamed them her "Broadway Als." Burns explained: "When we asked Ruby what the term meant, she told us that back in her chorus girl days, the 'Broadway Als' were the nice guys. They took the girls out after a show and never let them pay for anything." Burns added, "That's how we treated Ruby, so we were proud to be her 'Broadway Als.'"

Burns accompanied Ruby to one of the most outstanding tributes to her career on March 2, 1990. Warner Bros. threw itself a party, a "Celebration of Tradition." Produced by David Wolper, Jack Haley, Jr. (who also directed), and Steven Spielberg, the spectacular party commemorated Warner's reclaiming of its entire lot, which for the last 18 years it had co-owned in Burbank with Columbia Studios.

The Warner logo was once again proudly displayed on the studio's water tower. The evening was classic Hollywood—very sentimental and nostalgic. Ruby, the studio's first female musical star, was radiant. She remarked, "Reporters always ask how it used to be. After tonight, they won't have to ask anymore."

Ruby hosted the "Salute to Busby Berkeley" segment of the fabulous star-studded show. A clip of Berkeley's "By a Waterfall" number was shown and followed by a live reenactment. Ruby's sister Gertrude was introduced as one of the original Berkeley girls.

All in all, the evening was a musical journey through a fabled past. Ruby Keeler had come home again.

APPENDIX A

Ruby Keeler's Stage Shows

1. *The Rise of Rosie O'Reilly*, 1923

Producer: George M. Cohan
Starring: Mary Lawlow, George Bancroft
Ruby Keeler appeared in chorus (first professional stage
appearance)

2. *Bye, Bye, Bonnie*, 1927

Producer: Lawrence Weber
Writers: Bide Dudley, Louis Simon
Starring: Dorothy Burgess, William Frawley, Louis Simon,
Rudolph Cameron, Bernard Cavanaugh
New York Herald Tribune said: "Ruby Keeler pushes enough
personality across the footlights to make her worthy of the
price of admission."

3. *Lucky*, 1927

Producer: Charles Dillingham
Writers: Otto Harbach, Bert Kalmar, Harry Ruby, Jerome Kern
Musical direction: Paul Whiteman
Choreographers: David Bennett, Albertina Rasch
Starring: Mary Eaton, Walter Catlett, Joseph Santley, Ivy
Sawyer, Al Ochs, "Skeets" Gallagher
Reviews: "Ruby Keeler is a gem." "Ruby Keeler scores with her
tap dancing." "Ruby Keeler's magnificent speed as a dancer
is one of the show's advantages."

4. *The Sidewalks of New York*, 1927

Producer: Charles Dillingham
Written and directed by: Eddie Dowling, Jimmy Hanley
Music, lyrics: Eddie Dowling, Jimmy Hanley
Choreographer: Earl Lindsay
Staged by: Edgar MacGregor
Starring: Ray Dooley, Cecil Owen, Joe Smith, Charles Dale,
Harry Short, Gladys Ahern.
Reviews: "Ruby Keeler [is] a damsel whose dancing proclivities
are marked, to say the least." "[Ruby Keeler is an]
outstanding representative of the newer musical comedy
stars." "Performance got under way largely through the
influence of Ruby Keeler."

5. *Show Girl*, 1929

Producer: Florenz Ziegfeld
Writer/Dialogue: William A. McGuire
Based on the novel by J. P. McEvoy
Music: George Gershwin
Lyrics: Gus Kahn and Ira Gershwin
Dance director: Bobby Connolly
Ballets: Albertina Rasch
Sets: Joseph Urban
Costumes: John W. Harkrider
Orchestral direction: William Daly
Stage director: Zeke Colvan
Technical director: T. B. McDonald
Starring: Ruby Keeler Jolson; Clayton, Jackson and Durante;
    Austin Fairman; Frank McHugh; Eddie Foy, Jr.
Reviews: *Broadway Theatre Guild:* "It would not surprise us to
    find Ruby Keeler the next leading lady to gain the stellar
    position in musical comedy so long held by Marilyn Miller."
    "Ruby Keeler does her tap dancing to bursts of applause."
    "Ruby Keeler climbs high as a comedienne." "*Show Girl*
    proves smash hit in premiere."

6. *No, No, Nanette*, 1971

Producers: Lee Guber and Shelley Gross
Produced for Broadway stage by Cyma Rubin
Supervision: Busby Berkeley
Adapted and directed by Burt Shevelove, C. Hewett
Music: Vincent Youmans
Lyrics: Irving Caesar and Otto Harbach
Costumes: Sara Brook
Choreographer: Dan Siretta
Musical direction: William Cox
Starring: Ruby Keeler, Cyril Ritchard, Helen Gallagher, Bobby
    Van, Patsy Kelly, Susan Watson, Jack Gilford, Roger Rathburn
Reviews: "Ruby Keeler is better than ever—the house goes mad
    when she slams into her dance routines." "Keeler floats through
    the show with charm and warmth. She whisks the audience
    back to Busby Berkeley days." "Ruby Keeler wows critics—she
    injects joy and excitement into a bad theatre season."

APPENDIX B

Ruby Keeler's Films

1. *Ruby Keeler Movietone*
Studio and year: Fox, 1928
Starring: Ruby Keeler
Story: A 2-minute short testing the reproduction of the sound of tap-dancing on film. It was released to theatres to promote Fox's "Movietone" process.
Reviews: *Variety:* "Ruby Keeler, revue dancer, snapped through a short but nifty tap-dance. The machine gets every tap and reveals Miss Keeler as an exceptional female hoofer. She's dressed in form-fitting trunks with a blouse effect. Short but neat subject."

2. *42nd Street*
Studio and year: Warner Bros., 1933
Screenplay: James Seymour and Rian James, from the novel by Bradford Ropes
Director: Lloyd Bacon
Dance direction: Busby Berkeley
Cast: Warner Baxter, Bebe Daniels, George Brent, Una Merkel, Ruby Keeler, Guy Kibbee, Dick Powell, Ginger Rogers, George E. Stone, Robert McWade, Ned Sparks, Eddie Nugent, Allen Jenkins, Harry B. Walthall, Al Dubin, Harry Warren, Toby Wing, Pat Wing, Tom Kennedy, Walls Clark, Jack La Rue, Louise Beavers, Dave O'Brien, Patricia Ellis, George Irving, Charles Lane, Milton Kibbee, Rolfe Sedan, Lyle Talbot, Gertrude Keeler, Helen Keeler, Geraine Grear, Ann Hovey, Renee Whitney, Dorothy Coonan, Barbara Rogers, June Glory, Jayne Shadduck, Adele Lacey, Loretta Andrews, Margaret La Marr, Mary Jane Halsey, Ruth Eddings, Edna Callaghan, Patsy Farnum, Maxine Cantway, Lynn Browning, Donna Mae Roberts, Lorena Layson, Alice Jans
Story: Baxter plays the harried producer-director who tries to persuade inexperienced chorine Keeler to replace injured star Daniels. She does and, of course, is a smash. The famous line by Baxter has been used ever since: "You're going out there a youngster, but you're coming back a star."
Reviews: *Hollywood Reporter:* "Little Mrs. Al Jolson (Ruby Keeler) is a new, bright, shining musical comedy star." *New*

York Daily Mirror: "Appealing little Ruby Keeler [is] a new refreshing type to step before Hollywood's jaded cameras." *New York Times:* "Ruby Keeler's ingratiating personality, coupled with her dances and songs, adds to the zest of the film."

3. *Golddiggers of 1993*

Studio and year: Warner Bros., 1933
Screenplay: Erwin Gelsey and James Seymour, from the play *The Golddiggers* by Avery Hopwood
Dialogue: David Boehm and Ben Markson
Director: Mervyn LeRoy
Dance direction: Busby Berkeley
Cast: Ruby Keeler, Warren William, Joan Blondell, Aline MacMahon, Dick Powell, Guy Kibbee, Ned Sparks, Ginger Rogers, Clarence Nordstrom, Robert Agnew, Tammany Young, Sterling Holloway, Ferdinand Gottschalk, Lynn Browning, Charles C. Wilson, Billy Party, Fred Toones, Theresa Harris, Joan Barclay, Wallace MacDonald, Wilbur Mack, Grace Hayle, Charles Lane, Hobart Cavanaugh, Bill Elliott, Dennis O'Keefe, Busby Berkeley, Fred Kelsey, Frank Mills
Story: A group of insurance salesmen back a show. Keeler is an unemployed dancer and Powell is her singer-composer boyfriend.
Reviews: *Modern Screen Magazine:* "Ruby Keeler proves her hit in *42nd Street* was no accident."

4. *Footlight Parade*

Studio and year: Warner Bros., 1933
Screenplay: Manuel Seff and James Seymour
Director: Lloyd Bacon
Dance direction: Busby Berkeley
Cast: Ruby Keeler, James Cagney, Joan Blondell, Dick Powell, Guy Kibbee, Ruth Donnelly, Claire Dodd, Hugh Herbert, Frank McHugh, Arthur Hohl, Gordon Westcott, Renee Whitney, Philip Faversham, Juliet Ware, Herman Bing, Paul Porcasi, William Granger, Charles Wilson, Barbara Rogers, Billy Taft, Marjean Rogers, Pat Wing, Donna Mae

Roberts, Dave O'Brien, George Chandler, Robert
Cavanaugh, William Mong, Lee Moran, Billy Barter, Harry
Seymour, Sam McDaniel, Fred Kelsey, Jimmy Conlin,
Roger Gray, John Garfield, Duke York, Donna LaBarr
Story: Cagney is the producer of "movie prologues" (brief
song-and-dance skits once used in movie theatres before the
presentation of the movie feature). Keeler is one of his
secretaries who turns dancer. Powell is the singing lead.

5. Dames

Studio and year: Warner Bros., 1934
Screenplay: Delmer Daves, from a story by Daves and Robert
Lord
Director: Ray Enright
Dance direction: Busby Berkeley
Cast: Ruby Keeler, Joan Blondell, Dick Powell, ZaSu Pitts,
Guy Kibbee, Hugh Herbert, Arthur Vinton, Sammy Fain,
Phil Regan, Arthur Aylesworth, Lelia Bennett, Berton
Churchill
Story: Same old formula—finding backers for a musical. Keeler
and Powell are backstage lovers again. Keeler, daughter of
Kibbee and Pitts, secretly takes part in a show written by
Powell. Outstanding number is entire screen filled with
Keeler's face in a jigsaw puzzle design.

6. Flirtation Walk

Studio and year: Warner Bros./First National, 1934
Screenplay: Delmer Daves, from a story by Daves and Lou
Edelman
Director: Frank Borzage
Dance direction: Bobby Connolly
Cast: Ruby Keeler, Dick Powell, Pat O'Brien, Ross Alexander,
John Arledge, Henry O'Neill, Guinn Williams, Frederick
Burton, John Darrow, Glen Boles, Col. Tim Lonergan,
Gertrude Keeler, Tyrone Power, Lt. Joe Cummins, Cliff
Saum, Paul Fix, Sol Bright, William Worthington, Emmet
Vogan, Maude Turner Gordon, Frank Dawson, Frances Lee,
Avis Johnson, Mary Russell, Carlyle Blackwell, Jr., Dick
Winslow

Story: Musical set at West Point Military Academy. Keeler, an officer's daughter, falls in love with Cadet Powell.

7. Go Into Your Dance
Studio and year: Warner Bros./First National, 1935
Screenplay: Earl Baldwin, from a story by Bradford Ropes
Director: Archie L. Mayo
Dance direction: Bobby Connolly
Cast: Ruby Keeler, Al Jolson, Glenda Farrell, Helen Morgan, Barton MacLane, Sharon Lynne, Patsy Kelly, Benny Rubin, Phil Regan, Gordon Westcott, William Davidson, Joyce Compton, Akim Tamiroff, Joe Cregan
Story: Jolson is an actor-singer whose career has been ruined by drinking and gambling. Keeler is the chorus girl who saves him. A weak musical that was rushed into production so Jolson could appear with his wife.

8. Shipmates Forever
Studio and year: Warner Bros./First National, 1935
Screenplay: Delmer Daves
Director: Frank Borzage
Cast: Ruby Keeler, Dick Powell, Lewis Stone, Ross Alexander, Eddie Acuff, Richard Foran, John Arledge, Robert Light, Joseph King, Frederick Burton, Henry Kolker, Joseph Crehan, Mary Treen, Martha Merrill, Carlyle Moore, Henry Seymour
Story: Keeler is a Navy orphan who sings and dances her way into the heart of cocky Annapolis cadet Powell.

9. Colleen
Studio and year: Warner Bros., 1936
Screenplay: Peter Milne and F. Hugh Herbert, from a story by Robert Lord
Director: Alfred B. Green
Dance direction: Bobby Connolly
Cast: Ruby Keeler, Dick Powell, Jack Oakie, Joan Blondell, Hugh Herbert, Louise Fazenda, Paul Draper, Marie Wilson, Luis Alberni, Hobart Cavanaugh, Berton Churchill, J. M. Kerrigan, Spencer Charters, Addison Richards, Mary Treen, Charles Coleman

Story: A lesser known Warners musical with usual boy-meets-girl theme. This was the last of Keeler's film musicals with Powell.

10. *Ready, Willing and Able*
Studio and year: Warner Bros., 1937
Screenplay: Jerry Wald, Sig Herzig and Warren Duff, from a story by Richard Macaulay
Director: Ray Enright
Dance direction: Bobby Connolly
Cast: Ruby Keeler, Lee Dixon, Allen Jenkins, Louise Fazenda, Carol Hughes, Ross Alexander, Winifred Shaw, Teddy Hart, Hugh O'Connell, Addison Richards, Shaw and Lee, E. E. Clive, Jane Wyman, May Boley, Charles Halton, Adrian Rosley, Lillian Kemble Cooper, Barnett Parker
Story: Keeler persuades boyfriend O'Connell to put up the money for a show produced by Dixon and Alexander. She dances with Dixon (on the keys of a giant typewriter) and ends up with Alexander.

11. *Mother Carey's Chickens*
Studio and year: RKO, 1938
Screenplay: S. K. Lauren and Gertrude Purcell from the novel by Kate Douglas Wiggin and the play by Wiggin and Rachel Crothers
Director: Rowland V. Lee
Cast: Ruby Keeler, Anne Shirley, James Ellison, Fay Bainter, Walter Brennan, Frank Albertson, Donnie Dunagan, Alma Kruger, Jackie Moran, Phyllis Kennedy, Harvey Clark, Lucille Ward, George Irving
Story: In this non-musical, Keeler and Shirley are the daughters of widow Bainter, who keeps a boarding house patronized by school teachers. Small-budget film shown usually on a double bill.

12. *Sweetheart of the Campus*
Studio and year: Columbia, 1941
Screenplay: Robert D. Andrews and Edmund Hartmann, from a story by Andrews

Director: Edward Dmytryk
Cast: Ruby Keeler, Ozzie Nelson, Harriet Hilliard, Gordon
  Olivier, Don Beddoe, Charles Judels, Kathleen Howard,
  Byron Foulger, George Lessey, Frank Gaby, Leo Watson
  and the Four Spirits of Rhythm
Story: Keeler is a wisecracking chorus girl who starts a
  nightclub on a college campus. She returns to her lively
  singing and dancing in this one.

13. *The Phynx*

Studio and year: Warner Bros., 1970
Screenplay: Stan Cornyn, from a story by Bob Booker and
  George Foster
Director: Lee H. Katzin
Cast: A. Michael Miller, Ray Chippeway, Dennis Larden,
  Lonny Stevens, Lou Antonio, Mike Kellin, Michael Ansara,
  George Tobias, Joan Blondell, Larry Hankin, Teddy Eccles,
  Ultra Violet, Pat McCormick, Joseph Gazal, Bob Williams,
  Barbara Noonan, Rich Little, Sue Bernard, Ann Morrell,
  Sherry Miles
Cameo bits: Ruby Keeler, Busby Berkeley, Edgar Bergen and
  Charlie McCarthy, Xavier Cugat, Andy Devine, Louis
  Hayward, George Jessel, Patsy Kelly, Dorothy Lamour, Joe
  Louis, Guy Lombardo, Marilyn Maxwell, Butterfly
  McQueen, Pat O'Brien, Maureen O'Sullivan, Martha Raye,
  Ed Sullivan, Rudy Vallee, Clint Walker, Johnny Weismuller
Story: The attempt of a rock group to rescue film and stage
  stars from a mythical country behind the Iron Curtain. It
  was put into a few isolated theatres and then withdrawn
  from release.

INDEX